VOLUME I

NEW TESTAMENT

THE NEW COLLEGEVILLE BIBLE COMMENTARY

THE GOSPEL ACCORDING TO

MATTHEW

Barbara E. Reid, O.P.

SERIES EDITOR

Daniel Durken, O.S.B.

LITURGICAL PRESS

Collegeville, Minnesota

www.litpress.org

Nihil obstat: Robert C. Harren, *Censor deputatus.*
Imprimatur: ✠ John F. Kinney, Bishop of St. Cloud, Minnesota, August 30, 2005.

Design by Ann Blattner.

Cover illustration: *Genealogy of Jesus* by Donald Jackson. Natural hand-ground ink on calfskin vellum, 15-7/8" X 24-1/2." Copyright 2005 *The Saint John's Bible* and the Hill Museum & Manuscript Library at Saint John's University, United States of America.

Photos: pages 12, 28, 64, 87, 102, Corel Photos; page 145, Flat Earth Photos.

3	4	5	6	7	8	9

Library of Congress Cataloging-in-Publication Data

Reid, Barbara E.
 The Gospel according to Matthew / Barbara E. Reid.
  p. cm. — (The new Collegeville Bible commentary. New Testament ; v. 1)
 Summary: "Complete biblical texts with sound, scholarly based commentary that is written at a pastoral level; the Scripture translation is that of the New American Bible with Revised New Testament and Revised Psalms (1991)" —Provided by publisher.
 ISBN-13: 978-0-8146-2860-7 (pbk. : alk. paper)
 ISBN-10: 0-8146-2860-5 (pbk. : alk. paper)
 1. Bible. N.T. Matthew—Commentaries. I. Title. II. Series.

BS2575.53.R45 2005
226.2'077—dc22   2005002593

CONTENTS

1 Cor 13
Romans 12 } Handbook
Gal 5   } for living

ABBREVIATIONS

Books of the Bible

Acts—Acts of the Apostles
Amos—Amos
Bar—Baruch
1 Chr—1 Chronicles
2 Chr—2 Chronicles
Col—Colossians
1 Cor—1 Corinthians
2 Cor—2 Corinthians
Dan—Daniel
Deut—Deuteronomy
Eccl (or Qoh)—Ecclesiastes
Eph—Ephesians
Esth—Esther
Exod—Exodus
Ezek—Ezekiel
Ezra—Ezra
Gal—Galatians
Gen—Genesis
Hab—Habakkuk
Hag—Haggai
Heb—Hebrews
Hos—Hosea
Isa—Isaiah
Jas—James
Jdt—Judith
Jer—Jeremiah
Job—Job
Joel—Joel
John—John
1 John—1 John
2 John—2 John
3 John—3 John
Jonah—Jonah
Josh—Joshua
Jude—Jude
Judg—Judges
1 Kgs—1 Kings

2 Kgs—2 Kings
Lam—Lamentations
Lev—Leviticus
Luke—Luke
1 Macc—1 Maccabees
2 Macc—2 Maccabees
Mal—Malachi
Mark—Mark
Matt—Matthew
Mic—Micah
Nah—Nahum
Neh—Nehemiah
Num—Numbers
Obad—Obadiah
1 Pet—1 Peter
2 Pet—2 Peter
Phil—Philippians
Phlm—Philemon
Prov—Proverbs
Ps(s)—Psalms
Rev—Revelation
Rom—Romans
Ruth—Ruth
1 Sam—1 Samuel
2 Sam—2 Samuel
Sir—Sirach
Song—Song of Songs
1 Thess—1 Thessalonians
2 Thess—2 Thessalonians
1 Tim—1 Timothy
2 Tim—2 Timothy
Titus—Titus
Tob—Tobit
Wis—Wisdom
Zech—Zechariah
Zeph—Zephaniah

Other Abbreviations

Ant. — *Antiquities of the Jews*
Apoc. Bar. —Syriac Greek Apocalypse
   of Baruch
H.E.—Eusebius, *Historia Ecclesiastica*
KJV—King James Version

LXX—Septuagint
Mart. Isa. —*Martyrdom of Isaiah*
NAB—New American Bible
T. Moses — *Testament of Moses*

The Gospel According to Matthew

In many ways the Gospel of Matthew holds primacy of place for Christians. It is the first book in the New Testament, and in patristic times it was thought to have been the first Gospel written. It was the Gospel most used in worship in the early church. And it has been the one most commented upon and preached, beginning with the first known commentary on the Gospel of Matthew by Origen (ca. A.D. 185–254).

Some of the best-loved passages in Scripture, as well as some of the most difficult sayings and teachings of Jesus, are found in this Gospel. This Gospel is distinctive for its emphasis on the Jewishness of Jesus, as authoritative teacher, whose life and ministry fulfill the Scriptures. Wisdom motifs also mark Matthew's presentation of Jesus. The assurance that Jesus is Emmanuel, "God-with-us," frames the whole Gospel (1:23; 28:20).

Author

Traditionally, the author of the First Gospel has been identified as Matthew, the tax collector who was called by Jesus (Matt 9:9) and sent out as an apostle (10:3). But, like many ancient authors, the evangelist nowhere identifies himself. The apostle Matthew may have been responsible for an earlier stage of the Gospel tradition, or he may have been a missionary to the area where this Gospel was composed. But most scholars agree that he was not the author of the Gospel. The composer copied extensively from the Gospel of Mark; an eyewitness would have told the story in his own words. It is also doubtful that a tax collector would have the kind of religious and literary education needed to produce this Gospel. Finally, the theological concerns in this Gospel are those of second-generation Christians. For the sake of brevity, however, we continue to refer to the author as "Matthew."

The evangelist was likely a Jewish Christian, writing for a community that was predominantly Jewish Christian. The author had extensive knowledge of the Hebrew Scriptures and a keen concern for Jewish observance and the role of the Law. A few scholars hold that Matthew was a Gentile because of his fierce anti-Jewish polemic, especially in chapter 23. In addition, he seems to have been unfamiliar with distinctions between Pharisees and Sadducees (e.g., 16:5-12; 22:23). He also appears to have misunderstood the Hebrew parallelism in Zechariah 9:9, thinking that the prophet is speaking of two beasts (21:1-9).

These, however, are not sure indicators that the evangelist was a Gentile. The anti-Jewish polemic can be explained as part of a Jewish Christian's attempt to define his community in relation to other Jews who have not followed Jesus. Matthew's juxtaposition of "Pharisees and Sadducees" is simply a generic phrase for the religious leaders at a time when Sadducees were no longer functioning. And the apparent misinterpretation of Zechariah 9:9 does not negate the evidence that the evangelist had a thorough knowledge of the Hebrew Scriptures, seen in his frequent biblical citations and allusions.

Date

Allusions to the destruction of the temple in Jerusalem (21:41-42; 22:7; 24:1-2) indicate that Matthew wrote after A.D. 70. A date of approximately A.D. 85 would allow time for circulation of the Gospel of Mark, one of Matthew's sources, which was composed close to A.D. 70.

Setting

We do not know the precise locale of the Matthean community, but a prosperous urban setting is likely from the twenty-six times that Matthew uses the word *polis*, "city" (cf. Mark, four times; Luke, sixteen times) and the twenty-eight times he mentions gold and silver (cf. Mark, one time; Luke, four times). Matthean Christians, like those of other locales, were women and men of diverse social and civic status, ethnic identities, and levels of wealth. They comprised only a small percentage of the total population. It was a mixed community of Jews and Gentiles, striving to work out their identity as the New Israel.

The oldest tradition, and still the most frequently suggested locale for the Matthean community, is Antioch of Syria. As the third largest city of the empire, it had a sizable Jewish population. It was an important center of emerging Christianity (Acts 11:19-26; 13:1-3), where Jewish and Gentile Christians struggled to work out their new relationship in Christ (Gal 2:11-13). Other possible settings include Caesarea Maritima, Sepphoris, Alexandria, Edessa, Tyre, and Sidon.

Jews and Christians

The relationship of the Matthean community to their Jewish counterparts is not entirely clear. Pointing to a rupture between the two groups are references to "their synagogues" (4:23; 9:35; 10:17; 12:9; 13:54), "your synagogues" (23:34), "their scribes" (7:29), "the Jews to the present [day]" (28:15), Jewish persecution of Jesus' followers (10:17; 23:34), and bitter denunciation of the scribes and Pharisees (ch. 23). There are stories of exemplary faith of those who are not Jews: the magi (2:1-12); a Roman centurion (8:5-13); a Canaanite woman (15:21-28); a Roman soldier (27:54). That Jesus' message is for Gentiles is seen clearly in the final commission (28:19) and more subtly in the inclusion of Ruth and Rahab in Jesus' genealogy (1:5); the coming of the magi to worship Jesus (2:11); the saying "in his name the Gentiles will hope" (12:21); the faith of a Canaanite woman (15:21-28); and in the parables of the tenants (21:33-43) and the marriage feast (22:1-10).

Yet, at the same time Matthew stresses a specific outreach to Israel. Only in Matthew does Jesus tell his disciples to confine their mission to the towns of Israel (10:5-6, 23; 15:24). And Matthew's Gospel, overall, is strongly Jewish in tone, emphasizing the abiding validity of the Law and fulfillment of the Scriptures.

This Gospel is designed to offer Matthew's Jewish Christians an account of Jesus' life and mission that enables them to relate to the two loyalties that pull them. On the one hand, they are Jews who are trying to define themselves in relation to other Jews who have not accepted Jesus. The latter see them as disloyal to the Mosaic covenant, engaged in dangerous partnership with pagans. On the other hand, they are Christians trying to relate to a community in which the majority is now Gentile, for whom the continued adherence of Jewish Christians to Jewish Law and customs would prove problematic. Matthew's Gospel tries to defend and define Jewish Christianity, on the one hand, and unity with Gentile Christians, on the other. It validates the community's continuity with the past promises to Israel, while at the same time justifies their new allegiance to the person of Christ and his mission.

A prime pastoral concern is the impact that Christian use of the Gospel of Matthew has had on Jewish-Christian relations. Statements in the Gospel that reflect the historical tensions of an emerging Jewish Christian community struggling to define itself in relation to other Jews need to be clearly explained as such so that they are not used to fuel anti-Judaism in contemporary contexts.

Composition

Eusebius, our earliest source of information on Matthew, quotes Papias of Hierapolis (ca. A.D. 125) as saying, "Matthew compiled the Sayings *(logia)* in the Hebrew language, and everyone translated them as well as they could" (*H.E.* 3.39.16). Irenaeus and Origen understood Eusebius's statement to mean that Matthew composed the Gospel in Hebrew or Aramaic. There is no firm evidence, however, that Papias was in a position to know the facts of the evangelist's method of composition. Moreover, his statement is full of ambiguities, and there is no indisputable evidence from the Greek text of the Gospel that it was translated from a Hebrew or Aramaic original.

Most modern scholars think that Matthew relied on the Marcan tradition as one of his prime sources. Matthew has retained some 600 of Mark's 660 verses, often streamlining the story and converting narration into dialogue. He follows Mark more closely from chapter 13 onward than in the first twelve chapters. Matthew adds infancy narratives and resurrection appearance stories, and recasts Jesus' teaching into five large blocks of discourse. He adapts the story to his predominantly Jewish Christian community by omitting explanations of Jewish customs (e.g., Matt 15:2; cf. Mark 7:3-4). Matthew also emphasizes more explicitly Jesus' fulfillment of the Scriptures, often citing specific texts from the Old Testament, particularly from the prophet Isaiah (e.g., 3:3; 4:14; 8:17). He gives more attention to the question of the Law and its observance (5:17-48).

Matthew, as well as Luke, also used a source called "Q" (for *Quelle*, German for "source") for some two hundred sayings of Jesus. Although no copy of this collection of sayings has yet been found, its existence can be supposed, due to the similarity in the wording and order of these sayings in the two Gospels. Finally, Matthew also relied on oral and written traditions, designated "M," that are unique to his Gospel.

The evangelist's own words capture well his method of composition: "every scribe who has been instructed in the kingdom of heaven is like the head of a household who brings from his storeroom both the new and the old" (13:52). Matthew both faithfully transmits and creatively shapes the tradition.

Structure

There are various ways to delineate the structure of Matthew's Gospel. Many think that Matthew's organizing principle was to present Jesus as the New Moses, giving five blocks of teaching, corresponding to the five books of the Pentateuch. A concluding formula, "When Jesus finished these words" (7:28; 19:1; cf. 11:1; 13:53; 26:1), marks off each section of narrative and discourse. Framing the whole are the infancy narratives and the passion-resurrection account. Benjamin W. Bacon was the first to propose this structure (*Studies in Matthew* [London: Constable, 1930]):

I. Infancy Narratives: 1:1–2:23
II. Five Books of Narratives and Discourses
    1. The Son Begins to Proclaim the Kingdom
        A. Narrative: Beginnings of the Ministry: 3:1–4:25
        B. Discourse: The Sermon on the Mount: 5:1–7:29
    2. The Mission of Jesus and His Disciples in Galilee
        A. Narrative: The Cycle of Nine Miracle Stories: 8:1–9:38
        B. Discourse: The Mission, Past and Future: 10:1–11:1
    3. Jesus Meets Opposition from Israel
        A. Narrative: Jesus Disputes with Israel: 11:2–12:50
        B. Discourse: Parables: 13:1-53
    4. The Messiah Forms the Church and Prophesies His Passion
        A. Narrative: The Itinerant Jesus Prepares for the Church by
            His Deeds: 13:54–17:27
        B. Discourse: Church Life and Order: 18:1-35
    5. The Messiah and the Church on the Way to the Passion
        A. Narrative: Jesus Leads His Disciples to the Cross
            as He Confounds His Enemies: 19:1–23:29
        B. Discourse: The Last Judgment: 24:1–25:46
III. Climax: Passion, Death, and Resurrection: 26:1–28:20

One problem with this structure is that it relegates the infancy and passion narratives to a marginal position, when, in fact, they are central to Matthew's story. Not all scholars agree that the motif of Jesus as the New Moses is the central organizing theme.

Some scholars see a chiastic pattern, with chapter 13 as the hinge (e.g., Peter Ellis, *Matthew: His Mind and His Message* [Collegeville: Liturgical Press, 1974]):

a   Narratives   chs. 1–4
  b   Sermons   chs. 5–7
    c   Narratives   chs. 8–9
      d   Sermons   ch. 10
        e   Narratives   chs. 11–12
          f   Sermon   ch. 13
        e'   Narratives   chs. 14–17
      d'   Sermons   ch. 18

    c'   Narratives   chs. 19–22

  b'   Sermons   chs. 23–25

a'   Narratives   chs. 26–28

In this configuration, Matthew 13:35 is the turning point: before it Jesus addresses all Jews; after it he devotes his attention solely to those who have already become his disciples.

Not all scholars see Matthew's structure in such neat patterns. Another approach is to regard Matthew more as a storyteller whose structure has more seams and turns and is determined by his retelling of Mark's story (e.g., Donald Senior, *What Are They Saying About Matthew?* [rev. ed.; New York/Mahwah: Paulist Press, 1996] 34–37):

    I. 1:1–4:11 Origin of Jesus

   II. 4:12–10:42 Galilean ministry of teaching (chs. 5–7) and healing (chs. 8–9) as a model for disciples' ministry (ch. 10)

 III. 11:1–16:12 Varying responses to Jesus (rejection by Jewish opponents, faith of disciples)

 IV. 16:13–20:34 Jesus and his disciples on the way to Jerusalem

  V. 21:1–28:15 Jerusalem; Jesus' final days of teaching in the temple

 VI. 28:16-20 Finale: Back to Galilee; disciples sent to the whole world; Jesus' abiding presence

This outline delineates the major movements and theological motifs of the Gospel, taking into account the fluid nature of narrative, and is the outline adopted in this commentary.

Purpose

This Gospel, with its emphasis on Jesus as authoritative Teacher and its stress on the ethical implications of discipleship, is a powerful catechetical tool. The evangelist may have composed it with the idea of providing a handbook for church leaders to assist them in preaching, teaching, and leading worship. This text is a particularly useful guide for helping believers discern what to keep from tradition and what to let go in changing circumstances. Its strategies for peace-making, reconciliation, and formation of community make this Gospel a potent pastoral aid. In every age it continues to bring new vision and hope to Christians in mission, inviting them into ever deeper relationship with Jesus, who remains always with them (1:23; 28:20).

The commentaries in this booklet are all primarily based on the Greek text rather than the New American Bible translation. Accordingly, the translation of words or phrases in the commentaries sometimes differs from the translation provided at the top of the page. It is hoped that these complementary translations will enhance understanding of the Gospel.

The Gospel According to Matthew

I. The Infancy Narrative

1 **The Genealogy of Jesus.** ¹The book of the genealogy of Jesus Christ, the son of David, the son of Abraham.

²Abraham became the father of Isaac, Isaac the father of Jacob, Jacob the father of Judah and his brothers. ³Judah became the father of Perez and Zerah,

THE ORIGINS OF JESUS

Matt 1:1–4:11

The opening chapters set the stage for the whole Gospel. Matthew, like Luke, begins with two introductory chapters of infancy narratives. The differences between the two accounts indicate that they did not share the same sources for this portion of the story. Matthew tells the story of Jesus' origins, the unusual circumstances surrounding his birth, and the threat to Jesus' life by Herod from the perspective of Joseph. Luke, in contrast, makes Mary central. Beginning with the infancy narratives, Matthew calls attention to the fulfillment of Scripture through Jesus' life and ministry. In the opening two chapters he highlights Jesus' Davidic descent and presents Jesus as recapitulating in his own life important events in the history of Israel. Matthew then situates Jesus in relation to John the Baptist, followed by his account of Jesus' testing in the desert in preparation for his public ministry.

1:1 Book of origins

The title verse introduces motifs that run throughout the whole of the Gospel. The opening phrase, "book of the genealogy *(biblos geneseōs)*," can also be translated "account of the birth" or "book of origin." This same phrase begins the account of creation in Genesis 2:4 (LXX) and the list of descendants of Adam in Genesis 5:1. Matthew narrates a new creative act of God. Three important titles follow. Jesus is *christos*, "messiah," the "anointed" of God. This term designates one who is set apart by God for particular service, such as kings (Pss 2:2; 89:20); priests (Lev 4:3, 5); prophets (1 Kgs 19:16). Some Jewish writings spoke of a coming messiah who would

11

whose mother was Tamar. Perez became the father of Hezron, Hezron the father of Ram,[4] Ram the father of Amminadab. Amminadab became the father of Nahshon, Nahshon the father of Salmon, [5]Salmon the father of Boaz, whose mother was Rahab. Boaz became the father of Obed, whose mother was Ruth. Obed became the father of Jesse,[6] Jesse the father of David the king.

David became the father of Solomon, whose mother had been the wife of Uriah. [7]Solomon became the father of Rehoboam, Rehoboam the father of Abijah, Abijah the father of Asaph. [8]Asaph became the father of Jehoshaphat, Jehoshaphat the father of Joram, Joram the father of Uzziah. [9]Uzziah became the father of Jotham, Jotham the father of Ahaz, Ahaz the father of Hezekiah. [10]Hezekiah became the father of Manasseh, Manasseh the father of Amos, Amos the father of Josiah. [11]Josiah became the father of Jechoniah and his brothers at the time of the Babylonian exile.

carry out God's purposes in a new way. Expectations surrounding this figure were by no means uniform. "Son of David," one of Matthew's favorite designations of Jesus (1:1, 20; 9:27; 12:23; 15:22; 20:30, 31; 21:9, 15; 22:42-45), underscores Jesus' royal status and also recalls God's choice of unlikely persons for important roles in salvation history. "Son of Abraham" relates Jesus to the prime figure in Israel's history, the one whose struggle to be obedient to God brought blessing for all the peoples on earth.

1:2-17 The genealogy of Jesus (cf. Luke 3:23-38)

The genealogy functions not as a historical record but as a way to situate Jesus in relation to the memorable characters in Israel's history. It tells who he is by recounting who his people are. Drawing on 1 Chronicles 1:28-42; 3:5-24; Ruth 4:12-22, Matthew outlines Jesus' ancestors in three schematized sections of fourteen generations each (v. 17). The progression is from Israel's origin in Abraham to its glorious days under David (vv. 2-6a), then to the disastrous time of the Babylonian exile (vv. 6b-11), and finally to the hope-filled future with the birth of the Messiah (vv. 12-16). The number fourteen is symbolic. Some think that it represents the numerical value of the name David (d + v + d = 4 + 6 + 4 = 14), but more likely it signifies fullness or completion, being double the number seven, which symbolizes perfection in the Bible. A problem is that the last section has only thirteen generations. Matthew simply may have miscounted, or a name may have dropped out in the transmission.

The linear progression of thirty-nine male ancestors is broken at four points by the names of women. They are not the ones who would immediately come to mind as great figures from Israel's past. Each has an unusual twist to her story. Tamar (v. 3), after being widowed, took decisive

13

Modern Nazareth and the Basilica of the Annunciation

¹²After the Babylonian exile, Jechoniah became the father of Shealtiel, Shealtiel the father of Zerubbabel, ¹³Zerubbabel the father of Abiud. Abiud became the father of Eliakim, Eliakim the father of Azor, ¹⁴Azor the father of Zadok. Zadok became the father of Achim, Achim the father of Eliud, ¹⁵Eliud the father of Eleazar. Eleazar became the father of Matthan, Matthan the father of Jacob, ¹⁶Jacob the father of Joseph, the husband of Mary. Of her was born Jesus who is called the Messiah.

¹⁷Thus the total number of generations from Abraham to David is fourteen generations; from David to the Babylonian exile, fourteen generations; from the Babylonian exile to the Messiah, fourteen generations.

The Birth of Jesus. ¹⁸Now this is ► how the birth of Jesus Christ came

action to coerce her father-in-law, Judah, to provide an heir for her (Gen 38). She conceived Perez and Zerah, who continued the Davidic line. Tamar is the only woman in the Hebrew Scriptures who is called righteous (Gen 38:26), a term that is of central importance to Matthew. Rahab (v. 5), a prostitute in Jericho (Josh 2), risked disobeying the orders of the king of Jericho and sheltered spies sent from Joshua to reconnoiter the land. She subsequently gave birth to Boaz, the great-grandfather of David. Ruth (v. 5), a Moabite woman, returned with her mother-in-law, Naomi, to Bethlehem, rather than stay with her own people after her husband Mahlon died. In Bethlehem, Ruth presented herself to Boaz at the threshing floor and conceived Obed, who carried forth the Davidic line. Finally, the wife of Uriah (v. 6) is the one who bore David's son Solomon after David arranged to have Uriah killed in battle (2 Sam 11).

Each story speaks of how women took bold actions outside the bounds of regular patriarchal marriage to enable God's purposes to be brought to fruition in unexpected ways. Not only were the circumstances unusual, but some of these women were also outsiders to Israel. Remembering their stories prepares for the extraordinary circumstances of Jesus' birth and the salvation he will ultimately extend to those outside Israel (28:19). The women's presence in the midst of the male ancestors of Jesus also signals the integral role that women disciples play in the community of Jesus' followers. They remind the reader that women are not marginal to the history of Israel or of Christianity.

1:18-25 The birth of Jesus

Both the genealogy and the account of the birth of Jesus stress the theme of continuity and discontinuity. The same faithful God of Israel

► This symbol indicates a cross reference number in the *Catechism of the Catholic Church*. See page 155 for number citations.

about. When his mother Mary was betrothed to Joseph, but before they lived
together, she was found with child
through the holy Spirit. [19]Joseph her
husband, since he was a righteous man,
yet unwilling to expose her to shame,
decided to divorce her quietly. [20]Such
was his intention when, behold, the
angel of the Lord appeared to him in a
dream and said, "Joseph, son of David,
do not be afraid to take Mary your wife
into your home. For it is through the
holy Spirit that this child has been conceived in her. [21]She will bear a son and
you are to name him Jesus, because he
will save his people from their sins."
[22]All this took place to fulfill what the
Lord had said through the prophet:

---

continues to act with saving grace toward the New People of God in sur-
prising ways. Verses 18-25 explain how Jesus is son of God through the
holy Spirit and "son of David" through legal adoption by Joseph.

Marriage in first-century Palestine, usually arranged by the elders of
the two families, took place in two steps. There was a formal betrothal before witnesses that was legally binding. The bride remained in her
father's home for another year or so until the ceremony of her transfer to
the home of her husband. Jesus' conception occurs between these two
stages. The agency of the holy Spirit (v. 18) is not sexual; rather, the Spirit
is God's life-giving power evident in creation (Gen 1:2; Ps 104:30) and in
prophetic speech (22:43). It is the divine power at work in Jesus (3:16;
12:18, 28) and his disciples (10:20).

Joseph is faced with an impossible dilemma (v. 19). He is a righteous
(dikaios) man, that is, one who is faithful to the demands of the Law. The
Law prescribed death for adulterers (Deut 22:23-27). But Joseph is unwilling to publicly denounce his betrothed. A secret divorce is not possible;
two witnesses are needed, and Mary's pregnancy would be known by all
her relatives and townspeople. Joseph decides on a middle course: he will
divorce her quietly (Deut 24:1), without stating the reasons. He will not initiate a public trial (Num 5:11-31). This solution, however, does not prevent
Mary from being exposed to public shame. The only way to prevent this
would be for Joseph to complete his marriage to her and adopt the child as
his own. This is what the angel instructs him to do in a dream (v. 20).

This is the first of four instances in the infancy narratives in which an
angel communicates with Joseph through a dream (see also 2:13, 19, 22).
This is a common means of divine revelation in biblical tradition (see Gen
16:7-14; 37:5-11), especially to announce the birth of important figures in
Israel's salvation (Ishmael, Gen 16:7-12; Isaac, Gen 17:1-19; Samson, Judg
13:3-22). There are usually five elements in annunciations: (1) the angel
appears; (2) the person is afraid; (3) the angel gives reassurance, announces

23"Behold, the virgin shall be with
child and bear a son,
and they shall name him
Emmanuel,"

which means "God is with us." ²⁴When
Joseph awoke, he did as the angel of
the Lord had commanded him and
took his wife into his home. ²⁵He had

---

the birth, tells the child's name and its meaning, and foretells his great
deeds; (4) the person objects; (5) the angel gives a sign. The angel assures
Joseph (v. 20) that this child is of God, and not from any act of unfaithfulness. God asks Joseph and Mary to complete their commitment to each
other in difficult circumstances. But they also have the promise that God
will be with them throughout (v. 23). The angel pronounces and interprets
the name of the child, Jesus (v. 21). This derivative of the name Joshua (in
Hebrew, *Yeshua* or *Yeshu*) was common in the first century. It means "God
helps" but came to be associated with the verb *yš^c*, which means "God
saves." Jesus' saving mission of forgiveness is enacted in healing stories
(9:2-8) and is confirmed in his words to his disciples at his final supper
with them (26:28).

The first of Matthew's quotations of the Hebrew Scriptures (vv. 22-23)
is from Isaiah 7:14. As in 2:15, 17, 23; 4:14; 8:17; 13:35; 21:4; 26:56; 27:9, the
citation begins with the formula "this took place to fulfill what the Lord
had said through the prophet" (see also the Old Testament citations without this exact formula in 2:5; 3:3; 12:17; 13:14). In Isaiah 7:14 the oracle to
King Ahaz refers to the birth of a royal son in the near future who will be
a sign of hope to Judah. The Hebrew word *^calmâ*, "young woman," refers
to the mother's age, not her sexual status (*betulah* is the Hebrew word for
"virgin"). The Septuagint, the Greek translation, however, renders this
parthenos, "virgin." Isaiah is predicting a birth that will come about in a
normal way, but Matthew applies it to the virginal conception of Jesus.
The promise of Emmanuel, "God is with us" frames the whole Gospel
(1:23; cf. 28:20).

Joseph follows the angel's commands and completes the marriage
ceremony with Mary (v. 24) and names her son Jesus (v. 25). Again Matthew underscores Mary's virginity at the time of Jesus' conception and
birth. Verse 25 is ambiguous; it neither affirms nor denies Mary's perpetual virginity.

In this opening chapter Jesus' identity is established in relation to God,
to the royal line of David, and to notable figures of Israel's past. He embodies the faithfulness and startling creativity of God, the kingliness of
David, and the bold and socially questionable righteousness of the

no relations with her until she bore a son, and he named him Jesus.

2 **The Visit of the Magi.** ¹When Jesus was born in Bethlehem of Judea, in the days of King Herod, behold, magi from the east arrived in Jerusalem, ²saying, "Where is the newborn king of the Jews? We saw his star at its rising and have come to do him homage." ³When King Herod heard this, he was greatly troubled, and all Jerusalem with him. ⁴Assembling all the chief priests and the scribes of the people, he inquired of them where the Messiah was to be born. ⁵They said to him, "In Bethlehem of Judea, for thus it has been written through the prophet:
⁶'And you, Bethlehem, land of Judah,
    are by no means least among the
        rulers of Judah;
since from you shall come a ruler,
    who is to shepherd my people
        Israel.'"

women in his ancestry and of his legal father, Joseph. In the next chapter the focus is on positive and negative responses to Jesus. Place names figure prominently, linking Jesus with significant events of Israel's history.

2:1-12 Herod and the magi

Matthew does not relate details about Jesus' birth (cf. Luke 2:1-7). What is of interest is the place and the initial reactions to him. Jesus' birth in Bethlehem, the place where David was anointed king (1 Sam 16:1-13), highlights his royal Davidic identity. The reigning king is Herod the Great, who was appointed by the Roman senate to rule Judea in 40 B.C. A power struggle will ensue between Jesus and the Herodian kings over who bears the title "king of the Jews" (v. 2; see 27:11, 29, 37, 42).

The first visitors to the newborn Jesus are exotic characters from the East. The term "magi" originally referred to a caste of Persian priests, who served their king. They were not kings or wise men, but were adept at interpreting dreams. Here they appear to be astrologers who can interpret the movement of the stars. Magi were often associated with sorcery and magic, and were not always held in high regard (e.g., the magicians of Pharaoh, Exod 7–8). Matthew, however, portrays them very favorably. These Gentiles who respond positively to Jesus stand in stark contrast to Herod, the chief priests, and scribes (v. 4), foreshadowing the inclusion of non-Jews in the Jesus movement and the rejection of Jesus by many Jews.

There is much speculation whether the episodes in Matthew 2 have a historical basis or whether they are creations of Matthew to serve his theological purposes. With regard to the star, some think it was Halley's comet, which appeared in 12–11 B.C., others the convergence of Jupiter and Saturn in 7–6 B.C. Alternatively, Matthew may have created it in

⁷Then Herod called the magi secretly and ascertained from them the time of the star's appearance. ⁸He sent them to Bethlehem and said, "Go and search diligently for the child. When you have found him, bring me word, that I too may go and do him homage." ⁹After their audience with the king they set out. And behold, the star that they had seen at its rising preceded them, until it came and stopped over the place where the child was. ¹⁰They were overjoyed at seeing the star, ¹¹and on entering the house they saw the child with Mary his mother. They prostrated themselves and did him homage. Then they opened their treasures and offered him gifts of gold, frankincense, and myrrh. ¹²And having been warned in a dream not to return to Herod, they departed for their country by another way.

---

conformity with the belief in antiquity that royal births are marked by astrological phenomena. Or Matthew may have intended an allusion to the story of Balaam, a sorcerer from the East, who predicted that a star would come out of Jacob (Num 24:17).

The Scripture quotation in verse 6 is a conflation of Micah 5:1 and 2 Samuel 5:2. Matthew customarily adapts the biblical citations to fit his context and purposes. As Jesus' birthplace, Bethlehem is no longer "too small to be among the clans of Judah" (Mic 5:1), but now is "by no means least among the rulers of Judah" (Matt 2:6). And just as God called David from Bethlehem to shepherd Israel (2 Sam 5:2), so Jesus is shepherd to God's people (9:36; 26:31).

The response of the magi to Jesus matches that of disciples. The magi are overjoyed at the sign of Jesus' birth (2:10), just as disciples' initial acceptance of Jesus is marked by joy (13:20, 44) and is promised as an end-time reward (25:21, 23). The magi bow down in homage to Jesus (v. 11; cf. Herod's insincere desire to do so in v. 8), as do the disciples after the storm (14:33), the Canaanite woman pleading for her daughter (15:25), and the women disciples (28:9) and the Eleven (28:17) when they meet the risen Christ. The magi give to Jesus the most precious gifts they have (v. 11), just as disciples offer him their very selves (4:22; 8:15; 10:37-39). Finally, the magi, like Joseph, are obedient to divine commands conveyed in dreams (v. 12), just as disciples are to obey the covenant and Jesus' word (5:19).

The text does not say how many magi there were or exactly from where they came. The traditional number of three magi is derived from the three gifts that they bear (2:11). It is possible that Matthew has in mind Psalm 72:10, which speaks of the kings of Arabia and Sheba bringing gifts to the newly anointed king. Or he may have intended an allusion to Isaiah

The Flight to Egypt. [13]When they had departed, behold, the angel of the Lord appeared to Joseph in a dream and said, "Rise, take the child and his mother, flee to Egypt, and stay there until I tell you. Herod is going to search for the child to destroy him." [14]Joseph rose and took the child and his mother by night and departed for Egypt. [15]He stayed there until the death of Herod, that what the Lord had said through the prophet might be fulfilled, "Out of Egypt I called my son."

The Massacre of the Infants. [16]When Herod realized that he had been deceived by the magi, he became furious. He ordered the massacre of all the boys in Bethlehem and its vicinity two years

---

60:6: "All from Sheba shall come / bearing gold and frankincense, / and proclaiming the praises of the LORD." In any case, Matthew sets the stage for all who will come from east and west to dine in the realm of God (8:11; 22:1-14).

2:13-15 The flight into Egypt

Each of the Gospels tells of those who not only reject Jesus but who actively seek to destroy him from the beginning of his ministry. Matthew begins this theme even earlier. From Jesus' very infancy Herod tries to kill him. As an intended victim of violence, the Matthean Jesus teaches his disciples how not to respond in kind to violence, to love their enemies, and to pray for their persecutors (5:38-48). There are circumstances, however, when flight is the necessary course of action (2:13-15).

Joseph takes center stage once again as he obediently fulfills the divine command conveyed in a dream (as also in 1:20-24; 2:19-20, 22). He takes Jesus and his mother to Egypt, a traditional place of refuge for Israelites (Gen 42–48; 1 Kgs 11:40; 2 Kgs 25:26; Jer 26:21; 41:16-18; 43:1-7).

The quotation from Hosea 11:1, "Out of Egypt I called my son" (2:15), seems odd, for the holy family is just going into Egypt. What Matthew presumes is that they will, indeed, leave Egypt, and by doing so Scripture is fulfilled in one more way. The text alludes to the Exodus and identifies Jesus with the paradigmatic saving event for Israel. Here begins Matthew's portrait of Jesus as a Moses-like figure, the authoritative Teacher of the Law.

2:16-18 The slaughter of the children

There is no verification of this event in historical records, but sources do attest to the cruelty of Herod. Josephus (*Ant.* 15; see also *T. Moses* 6:2-7) tells of how Herod, in his paranoia about his power, killed members of his own family. He also ordered the murder of one son from each of the leading

19

old and under, in accordance with the time he had ascertained from the magi. [17]Then was fulfilled what had been said through Jeremiah the prophet:

> [18]"A voice was heard in Ramah,
>   sobbing and loud lamentation;
> Rachel weeping for her children,
>   and she would not be consoled,
>   since they were no more."

The Return from Egypt. [19]When Herod had died, behold, the angel of the Lord appeared in a dream to Joseph in Egypt [20]and said, "Rise, take the child and his mother and go to the land of Israel, for those who sought the child's life are dead." [21]He rose, took the child and his mother, and went to the land of Israel. [22]But when he heard that Archelaus was ruling over Judea in place of his father Herod, he was afraid to go back there. And because he had been warned in a dream, he departed for the region of Galilee. [23]He went and dwelt in a town called Nazareth, so

---

families of Judea to ensure that there would be mourning at his funeral. The episode of the slaughter provides another parallel between Jesus and Moses, recalling Pharaoh's murder of the male Hebrew children (Exod 1:15-22). Just as God protected Moses through the actions of Moses' mother and sister and Pharaoh's daughter (Exod 2:1-10), so divine protection surrounds Jesus through the obedient actions of Joseph.

Once again, a citation from the Old Testament underscores the fulfillment of Scripture (2:17-18). Matthew adapts the quotation from Jeremiah 31:15 to fit his context and purpose. Rachel, who died en route from Bethel to Ephrath (which is identified with Bethlehem, Gen 35:16-21), is weeping for all the descendants of Israel who were marched off into exile. Ramah, about five miles north of Jerusalem, was on the route of the exile. Whereas Matthew uses this text to express the bitter lamentation of Israel over its slaughtered children, in Jeremiah it is part of an oracle that promises an end to the suffering and the return of the exiled Israelites (Jer 31:16).

2:19-23 A home in Nazareth

Just as Moses received a divine command to return home after the rulers who sought his life had died (Exod 4:19), so Joseph follows the angel's directive to go home to Israel with his family. Although Herod the Great is dead, his son Archelaus still poses a menace. Archelaus was the eldest of Herod's three sons among whom the kingdom was divided. He ruled Judea, Samaria, and Idumea for ten years (4 B.C.–A.D. 6), while Philip governed the area north and east of the Sea of Galilee, and Herod Antipas (14:1-12) controlled Galilee and Perea. Archelaus followed in his father's footsteps when it came to cruelty, but he did not have his father's administrative ability.

that what had been spoken through the prophets might be fulfilled, "He shall be called a Nazorean."

II. The Proclamation of the Kingdom

3 **The Preaching of John the Baptist.** ¹In those days John the Baptist appeared, preaching in the desert of Judea ²[and] saying, "Repent, for the kingdom of heaven is at hand!" ³It was

of him that the prophet Isaiah had spoken when he said:
"A voice of one crying out in the desert,
'Prepare the way of the Lord, make straight his paths.'"
⁴John wore clothing made of camel's hair and had a leather belt around his waist. His food was locusts and wild honey. ⁵At that time Jerusalem, all Judea, and the

---

Joseph, once again directed by a dream, takes his family to Galilee (2:22), which enjoyed greater peace than Judea. They settle in Nazareth, some four miles from the city of Sepphoris, which Herod Antipas was building as his capital. It is possible that the availability of work for Joseph, an artisan (13:55), was also a motivating factor for their choice of Nazareth as their new home. Matthew, however, sees this as one more way in which Scripture is fulfilled. There is actually no text in the Scriptures that says "He shall be called a Nazorean" (v. 23). Most likely Matthew sees a wordplay with *nēṣer*, "shoot" or "branch," and intends an allusion to Isaiah 11:1, "A shoot shall sprout from the stump of Jesse." This reference to a Davidic royal heir once again highlights Jesus' identity as king in the line of David (see Rom 15:12; 1 Pet 4:14; Rev 5:5, which also interpret Isaiah 11:1 in relation to Jesus as Messiah). Another possibility is that the wordplay is with *nāzîr*, meaning "one dedicated to God." Nazirites, like Samson (Judg 13:5-7), took a vow, did not cut their hair, and did not drink wine (Num 6:1-21) as a sign that they were set apart for God. Matthew may have in mind an allusion to Isaiah 4:3, "he . . . will be called holy." In any event, this final verse of the infancy narratives rounds out the portrait of Jesus as the fulfillment of all God's promises to Israel.

3:1-12 The proclamation of John the Baptist

The scene switches now to a desert area of Judea, east of Jerusalem, where John is baptizing and preaching repentance. The precise locale of John's ministry is not known. The arid region in the vicinity of the Dead Sea, along the Jordan River (3:6), is likely. John prepares the way, proclaiming the identical message as Jesus, "Repent, for the kingdom of heaven is at hand!" (3:2; 4:17).

The phrase "kingdom of heaven," unique to this Gospel, occurs thirty-two times. While Mark and Luke speak of the "kingdom of God," Matthew

whole region around the Jordan were going out to him ⁶and were being baptized by him in the Jordan River as they acknowledged their sins.

⁷When he saw many of the Pharisees and Sadducees coming to his baptism, he said to them, "You brood of vipers! Who warned you to flee from the coming wrath? ⁸Produce good fruit as evidence of your repentance. ⁹And do not presume to say to yourselves, 'We have Abraham as our father.' For I tell you, God can raise up children to Abraham from these stones. ¹⁰Even now the ax lies at the root of the trees. Therefore every tree that does not bear good fruit will be cut down and thrown into the fire. ¹¹I am baptizing you with water, for repentance, but the one who is coming after me is mightier than I.

"I am not worthy to carry his sandals. He will baptize you with the holy Spirit and fire. ¹²His winnowing fan is in his hand. He will clear his threshing

---

avoids using the divine name, much as Jews reading the Torah substitute "Adonai" ("Lord") for "YHWH." The expression "kingdom of heaven" does not connote a geographic area, nor does it refer to something that will be manifest only at a later time in the transcendent realm. The term *basileia*, "kingdom," means "kingly rule" or "reign," not a territory. God's reign is already present and visible here and now with the coming of Jesus (3:2; 4:17; 12:28), though it awaits completion (6:10, 33; 16:27-28).

In the context of first-century Palestine, this proclamation of God's reign was a direct challenge to Roman imperial authority. Jesus and John offer an alternate vision of power—not one based on domination and exploitation, but one in which forgiveness, healing, and well-being are offered to all. "God-with-us" means divine authoritative power over all and empowerment of all who become disciples. It is difficult to find an adequate way to express this in English. The metaphor "kingdom" falls short, evoking an image of male monarchical rule. Other ways to translate *basileia* include "rule," "reign," "realm," or "kin-dom," expressing this powerful and empowering relatedness of God's people in terms that are more inclusive.

John prepares people to recognize this embodiment of God's saving power in Jesus by adapting the words of the prophet Isaiah (40:3). In its original context the prophecy referred to the return of Israel from exile in Babylon, through the desert, to their homeland. Matthew also wants to portray John in the likeness of Elijah, with his ascetic clothing and diet (3:4; 2 Kgs 1:8). Many expected that Elijah would return as precursor and messenger before the end time (Mal 3:1; 4:5-6; Sir 48:10-11). Matthew makes this identification of John with Elijah even more explicit at 11:10, 14; 17:11-13.

With hyperbole, Matthew depicts the response to John as overwhelmingly positive (v. 5). The baptism John offers differs in several ways from

floor and gather his wheat into his barn, but the chaff he will burn with unquenchable fire."

The Baptism of Jesus. [13]Then Jesus came from Galilee to John at the Jordan to be baptized by him. [14]John tried to prevent him, saying, "I need to be baptized by you, and yet you are coming to me?" [15]Jesus said to him in reply, "Allow it now, for thus it is fitting

---

Jewish ritual washing: it is a one-time ritual, not repeated; it is not self-administered, but performed by God's prophet; and it is not for the removal of ritual impurity, but signifies repentance from sin (vv. 2, 6).

Unique to Matthew is the naming of Pharisees and Sadducees among those who come to John to be baptized (v. 7). The Pharisees were lay religious leaders active in Palestine from the second century B.C. until the first century A.D. Their name probably derives from the Hebrew word *perushîm*, "separated ones." They differed from the Sadducees in their oral interpretation of the Law, their more progressive theology, such as belief in resurrection (Matt 22:23; Acts 23:8), and in their accommodation to Hellenism. Sadducees were priests, from a more elite class, based in Jerusalem, whose role disappeared after the fall of the temple in A.D. 70. Their name may have come from the high priestly family of Zadok (1 Kgs 1:26) or from the word *ṣaddîqîm*, "just ones." The Sadducees had influence over the temple personnel and the political elite, whereas the Pharisees appealed to ordinary laypeople, advising them how to live everyday life in faithfulness to the Torah.

Matthew's introduction of these two groups of religious leaders brings onto the stage the prime opponents of Jesus. The Sadducees have a limited role in the Gospel, mentioned again only at 16:1, 6-12, while the Pharisees appear at every turn, challenging Jesus on his table practices (9:11; 15:1), fasting (9:14), the source of his power (9:34; 12:24), sabbath observance (12:2), and his interpretation of the Law (19:3). The Pharisees are the prime movers in the conspiracy to destroy Jesus (12:14; 21:46; 22:15). John's fierce accusation here reveals their insincerity in coming to be baptized and prepares for Jesus' denunciation of their hypocrisy in chapter 23. John insists that anyone who is serious about repentance must demonstrate this visibly in his or her deeds (v. 8), a theme in Jesus' teaching as well (7:21-23). Birth into the people of God is not sufficient for salvation (v. 9). A note of urgency is struck in verse 10. The time for producing "good fruit" (one of Matthew's favorite expressions; see 7:15-20; 12:33-37; 13:8, 22-26; 21:19, 43; 26:29) is now.

for us to fulfill all righteousness." Then he allowed him. ¹⁶After Jesus was baptized, he came up from the water and behold, the heavens were opened [for him], and he saw the Spirit of God descending like a dove [and] coming upon him. ¹⁷And a voice came from the heavens, saying, "This is my beloved Son, with whom I am well pleased."

After painting numerous parallels between John and Jesus, Matthew now clearly distinguishes the two (vv. 11-12). Jesus is more powerful than John; the baptizer is not even worthy to perform the task of a slave, to carry Jesus' sandals (v. 11). The reference to Jesus baptizing is best understood as a metaphor for his whole ministry of forgiveness, healing, and reconciliation. Only the Fourth Gospel mentions Jesus baptizing (John 3:22; 4:1-2).

Jesus' mission is one that refines with fire (see Zech 13:9; 1 Cor 3:13-15) and empowers people with the holy Spirit. And as a farmer separates wheat from chaff by tossing the harvested grain into the air with a winnowing fork, so Jesus will separate the righteous from the unrepentant at the end time (v. 12; see Jer 15:7). Unquenchable fire metaphorically expresses the unending pain of those whose choices separate them eternally from the love of God (similarly 13:30, 40-43, 49-50).

3:13-17 The baptism of Jesus

This episode further elaborates the relationship between Jesus and John and builds on the identification of Jesus as Son of God that was set forth in the infancy narratives. Only in Matthew's Gospel is there a dialogue between John and Jesus (vv. 14-15). It reflects the difficulties that the early Christians had with Jesus' undergoing John's baptism of repentance. First, if Jesus is greater than John (as John asserted in verse 11), then why does he appear subordinate here? A second problem is that as Christians came to believe in Jesus' sinlessness from birth, they struggled to explain why he would have sought John's baptism of repentance.

In Jesus' reply (v. 15) we find two key Matthean terms: "fulfill" and "righteousness." The theme of fulfillment of God's promises to Israel in the person of Jesus has been stressed from the outset with citations of Scripture (1:22-23; 2:5-6, 15, 17-18, 23) and in the way Jesus' life has replicated the history of his people. Matthew introduced his theme of righteousness when he applied the term to Joseph (1:19); now he affirms Jesus' righteousness. This is also a quality expected of disciples of Jesus (5:6, 10, 20; 6:33). The term *dikaiosynē*, "righteousness," denotes right relationship

4 **The Temptation of Jesus.** [1]Then Jesus was led by the Spirit into the desert to be tempted by the devil. [2]He fasted for forty days and forty nights, and afterwards he was hungry. [3]The tempter approached and said to him, "If you are the Son of God, command that these stones become loaves of bread." [4]He said in reply, "It is written:

'One does not live by bread alone,
but by every word that comes
forth from the mouth of
God.'"

[5]Then the devil took him to the holy city, and made him stand on the parapet of the temple, [6]and said to him, "If you are the Son of God, throw yourself down. For it is written:

---

with God, self, others, and all creation. From a Jewish perspective, righteousness is accomplished through faithfulness to the demands of the covenant, which the Matthean Jesus affirms (5:17-20).

A divine revelation further interprets the happening (vv. 16-17). "Rend[ing] the heavens" is a familiar expression from prophetic literature (Isa 63:19; cf. Ezek 1:1). People in Jesus' day imagined that the world is divided into three tiers: the heavens, the earth, and the underworld. An opening of the heavens signals a moment when human beings are in direct communication with the divine. The descent of the Spirit recalls the messianic prophecies of Isaiah: "the Spirit of the LORD shall rest upon him" (11:2; cf. 61:1) and "the spirit of God" that swept over the waters at creation (Gen 1:2; the Hebrew *rûaḥ ʾelohîm* can also be translated "a mighty wind," as in the NAB).

A heavenly voice (v. 17) is the counterpoint to the voice of John in the desert (v. 3). While in the Gospels of Mark (1:11) and Luke (3:22) the voice is directed only to Jesus: "*You* are my beloved Son," in Matthew the revelation is to all: "*This* is my beloved Son" (v. 17; emphasis added). This declaration carries multiple meanings. In the Hebrew Scriptures "son of God" occurs with three different nuances: (1) a chosen servant of God (the Hebrew *ʿebed*, "servant," is rendered *pais* in the LXX , which can also be translated "child") who will play a saving role for Israel and who will suffer for it (Isa 42:1; see 12:18-21, where Matthew explicitly presents Jesus as fulfilling this text); (2) a royal Davidic son (see Psalm 2:7, a coronation psalm, in which God assures the Davidic king, "You are my son"); (3) Israel is God's first-born son (Exod 4:22-23). The filial relationship between God and Israel is now personified in Jesus. There is also an echo of Genesis 22:2, where God instructs Abraham, "Take your son Isaac, your only one, whom you love" to the land of Moriah to offer him up. There is a foreshadowing that the sacrificial act that God interrupted with Isaac will be fulfilled with Jesus.

'He will command his angels concerning you'
and 'with their hands they will support you,
lest you dash your foot against a stone.'"

[7]Jesus answered him, "Again it is written, 'You shall not put the Lord, your God, to the test.'" [8]Then the devil took him up to a very high mountain, and showed him all the kingdoms of the world in their magnificence, [9]and he said to him, "All these I shall give to you, if you will prostrate yourself and worship me." [10]At this, Jesus said to him, "Get away, Satan! It is written:

'The Lord, your God, shall you worship
and him alone shall you serve.'"

[11]Then the devil left him and, behold, angels came and ministered to him.

Vivid metaphors of the heavens opening, the Spirit descending, and the voice of God speaking (see also 17:5) bring to a dramatic climax a scene that further establishes Jesus' identity as Son of God and Son of David. The baptism scene also points ahead to Jesus' death, where the centurion and his companions affirm, "Truly, this was the Son of God!" (Matt 27:54).

4:1-11 Testing in the wilderness

This is the final episode of the first section of the Gospel, which tells of Jesus' origins, establishes his identity, and sets the stage for the beginning of his public ministry. Matthew, like Luke (4:1-13), draws both from Mark's brief notice of Jesus' testing in the desert (Mark 1:12-13) and Q (see p. 8), which supplies a dialogue between Jesus and the devil. There is a mythical quality to the scene, as the evangelist has telescoped into one episode temptations that Jesus likely faced repeatedly throughout his life (Heb 4:15). There are also echoes of Israel's sojourn in the desert. But unlike Israel, who proved unfaithful during that time by grumbling against Moses, and testing God, Jesus stays steadfastly faithful to God's word. The fast for forty days and nights (v. 2) echoes that of Moses (Deut 9:18; so also Elijah, 1 Kgs 19:8). The motif of the mountain (v. 8) calls to mind Moses' encounter with God on Mount Sinai. Matthew uses this motif frequently (5:1–8:1; 15:29-31; 17:1-8; 28:16-20) to present Jesus as the authoritative interpreter of the Law.

While the first three chapters clearly establish Jesus' identity as "Son of God" for the reader, the tester (4:3) articulates three fundamental doubts. "*If* you are the Son of God . . ." (vv. 3, 6; emphasis added) functions both to confront the readers about any lingering doubts about what it means for Jesus to be beloved child of God and also demands that they examine

The Beginning of the Galilean Ministry. [12]When he heard that John had been arrested, he withdrew to Galilee. [13]He left Nazareth and went to live in Capernaum by the sea, in the region of Zebulun and Naphtali, [14]that what had been said through Isaiah the prophet might be fulfilled:

[15]"Land of Zebulun and land of
    Naphtali,

the way to the sea, beyond the
    Jordan,
Galilee of the Gentiles,
[16]the people who sit in darkness
    have seen a great light,
on those dwelling in a land over-
    shadowed by death
light has arisen."
[17]From that time on, Jesus began to preach and say, "Repent, for the kingdom of heaven is at hand."

---

their own answers to these tests as followers of God's own beloved. Each cuts to the core of what it means to be faithfully centered on God.

The first temptation is to be intent on gratifying one's own hungers (v. 3). Jesus counters with a quotation from Deuteronomy 8:3. In subsequent episodes Jesus enacts God's care for hungry people by feeding them with both physical and spiritual food (5:1–7:29; 14:31-21; 15:32-39; 26:26-30).

The second test concerns the desire for a showy display of power to prove God's might (v. 5). The devil takes Jesus to the parapet (literally, the "wing") of the temple and urges him to jump off to prove God's ability to rescue. He quotes Psalm 91, which assures that God's angels will let no evil befall the beloved. Jesus counters with another text from Deuteronomy (6:16). As the Gospel continues, Jesus remains true to his mission as "God-with-us," meeting people in their human needs and bringing them healing and empowerment. He does not compel people to believe through flashy displays of power, but in the paradoxical manner of God in human flesh.

The third test concerns idolatrous misuse of power (vv. 8-9). A human face is put on this temptation when Jesus makes the same reply, "Get away, Satan!" (v. 10), to Peter when he rejects Jesus' prediction of his passion (16:21-23). Here Jesus invokes Deuteronomy 6:13, bringing the focus again to true power and worship, which centers on God alone. The same verb, *proskyneō*, "prostrate," (v. 9) is used of the magi's adoration of the infant Jesus (2:2, 8), and of the women disciples' worship at the feet of the risen Christ (28:9).

Although the devil departs at the conclusion of this episode (v. 11), Matthew indicates that these tests haunted Jesus to the end. Even as he was dying a variation on these temptations surfaces: "He trusted in God; let him deliver him now if he wants him. For he said, 'I am the Son of God'" (27:43).

The Call of the First Disciples. [18]As he was walking by the Sea of Galilee, he saw two brothers, Simon who is called Peter, and his brother Andrew, casting a net into the sea; they were fishermen. [19]He said to them, "Come after me, and I will make you fishers of men." [20]At once they left their nets and followed him. [21]He walked along from there and saw two other brothers, James, the son of Zebedee, and his brother John. They were in a boat, with

The ministrations of angels (4:11) signal that divine protection and power always surround God's beloved ones, no matter how intense the trial.

THE BEGINNINGS OF THE GALILEAN MINISTRY

Matt 4:12–10:42

In the second main section of the Gospel, Matthew narrates the beginnings of Jesus' ministry in Galilee. After his opening proclamation of his mission (4:12-17), Jesus calls the first of his disciples (4:18-22) and begins to preach and heal multitudes of people (4:23-25). Then follows his magisterial teaching in the Sermon on the Mount (5:1–7:28), a series of healing stories (8:1–9:37), and the sending of the disciples in mission (10:1-42).

4:12-17 The announcement of the nearness of God's reign

Matthew, following Mark (1:14), links the beginning of Jesus' public ministry with John's arrest (4:12). He gives a fuller account of John's death at the hands of Herod Antipas at 14:3-12. It seems odd that Jesus would go to Galilee upon news of John's arrest; it may be that Jesus intended to take up the mission where John left off (see John 3:22-23; 4:1-3). The expression "withdrew to Galilee" (v. 12) clashes with Jesus' preaching in public (v. 17), and hints at the danger Jesus faces by ministering there.

Jesus resettles in Capernaum (see also 8:5; 9:1), a fishing village at the northwest corner of the Sea of Galilee. It lay along an important trade route, the *Via Maris*, "the Way of the Sea." This would have ensured a greater audience for his ministry than the tiny village of Nazareth (see 13:53-58, where Jesus is rejected in his hometown). For Matthew, the reason for Jesus' relocation is to fulfill Scripture (vv. 14-16). He adapts an oracle from the prophet Isaiah (9:1-2) to announce the hope that lies beyond death with the coming of Jesus. The oracle was originally addressed to Galilee after the Assyrian invasion in 732 B.C. To make the link, Matthew reminds the reader that Capernaum was in the general region of the territory allotted to the tribes of Zebulun and Naphtali (Josh 19:10-16; 19:32-39). The Matthean Jesus stresses at the outset that his mission is only to

29

Church of the Beatitudes on the western shore of the Sea of Galilee

their father Zebedee, mending their nets. He called them, ²²and immediately they left their boat and their father and followed him.

Ministering to a Great Multitude. ²³He went around all of Galilee, teaching in their synagogues, proclaiming the gospel of the kingdom, and curing every disease and illness among the people. ²⁴His fame spread to all of ▶ Syria, and they brought to him all who were sick with various diseases and

---

Israel (10:5; 15:24). But here again, as in the story of the magi (2:1-12), with the expression "Galilee of the Gentiles" (v. 15) there is a foreshadowing of the expansion of Jesus' mission to the Gentiles (28:16-20).

Jesus' opening proclamation of his mission (v. 17) matches that of John the Baptist (3:2). (See above, at 3:2, for comments on the meaning of "the kingdom of heaven.") The phrase "at hand" translates a word *(engiken)* that is ambiguous in Greek. It can mean "has arrived" or "has drawn near." Matthew (as also Mark 1:15) expresses that there is a new inbreaking of God's reign with the arrival of Jesus, but it is not yet fully accomplished. The expression "from that time on" (v. 17) marks an important transition in the story, as also at 16:21, where the phrase signals a new focus on Jesus' coming passion in Jerusalem.

4:18-22 The call of the first disciples

In this stylized account of the call of Jesus' first followers, Matthew introduces key characteristics of discipleship, which help readers reflect on their own response to Jesus. First, the invitation is initiated by Jesus. Unlike disciples of rabbis, who would seek out the one with whom they wanted to study, these disciples of Jesus are invited by him. They are going about their everyday work, casting their nets into the sea and making repairs to them when Jesus encounters them at the seaside. Far from being "uneducated, ordinary men," as the polemical reference to Peter and John in Acts 4:13 states, these fishermen were savvy businessmen who managed employees (Mark 1:20) and located their industry in an advantageous tax district. Philip and Andrew were originally from Bethsaida (John 1:44), in the territory ruled by Philip. It is likely that they relocated to Capernaum for a tax break.

Jesus' invitation is to an active mission. Discipleship does not entail merely intellectual assent, but following Jesus in every respect, becoming "fishers" of other persons (see Jer 16:16). There is a stress on the totality and immediacy of the response of these first disciples. The radical changes that the life of discipleship demands are symbolized in the leaving of their nets, their boat, and their father. In the story there is no preparation for this

racked with pain, those who were possessed, lunatics, and paralytics, and he cured them. ²⁵And great crowds from Galilee, the Decapolis, Jerusalem, and Judea, and from beyond the Jordan followed him.

encounter with Jesus. There is something so compelling about his person and message that Peter, Andrew, James, and John immediately follow him.

The communal dimension of discipleship is emphasized by the coming of the call to two sets of brothers. That the call can be rejected is shown in the story of the rich young man (19:16-22). The inclusion of marginalized people in Jesus' entourage is exemplified in the call of the toll collector Matthew (9:9-13). Others for whom there is no call story but who are clearly disciples of Jesus include the women "who had followed Jesus from Galilee, ministering to him" (27:55), among whom were "Mary Magdalene and Mary the mother of James and Joseph, and the mother of the sons of Zebedee" (27:56). Another latecomer in the Gospel is Joseph of Arimathea, whom Matthew also identifies as "a disciple of Jesus" (27:57).

4:23-25 The spreading of Jesus' fame

A summary statement of Jesus' successful ministry of teaching, preaching, and healing makes a bridge between the opening proclamation and initial formation of disciples to the advanced teaching (chs. 5–7) and further healing (chs. 8–9) that precede the sending out of the disciples on mission (ch. 10). Unlike the Gospel of John, which shows Jesus moving between Galilee and Jerusalem, in the Synoptic Gospels Jesus' ministry first centers only on Galilee (v. 23). He makes only one fateful trip to Jerusalem, which begins at Matthew 19:1. Characteristic of Matthew's emphasis on the primacy of Jesus' mission to Israel (10:5; 15:24) is that Jesus teaches in synagogues (v. 23). The expression "their synagogues" reflects the tension in Matthew's day between his predominantly Jewish Christian community and Jews who have not chosen to follow Jesus (see above, "Jews and Christians," in the introductory comments, p. 7).

The geographical sweep indicates those places from which Matthean Christians hailed or places in which the Gospel first circulated. Syria (v. 24) most likely refers to the Roman province by that name, which included Palestine and the other places listed in verse 25. "Decapolis, Ten Cities," most of which were on the east side of the Jordan River, were cities in which Hellenistic culture flourished and which were thought of as Gentile regions. The names thus hint at a mixture of Jews and Gentiles. This great multitude becomes the audience for Jesus' Sermon on the Mount.

5 **The Sermon on the Mount.** ¹When he saw the crowds, he went up the mountain, and after he had sat down, his disciples came to him. ²He began to teach them, saying:

The Beatitudes

³"Blessed are the poor in spirit,
　　for theirs is the kingdom of
　　　heaven.

⁴Blessed are they who mourn,
　　for they will be comforted.
⁵Blessed are the meek,
　　for they will inherit the land.
⁶Blessed are they who hunger and
　　　thirst for righteousness,
　　for they will be satisfied.
⁷Blessed are the merciful,
　　for they will be shown mercy.
⁸Blessed are the clean of heart,

THE SERMON ON THE MOUNT

Matt 5:1–7:28

This is probably the best known and most quoted part of the Gospel. Luke has a comparable sermon, but sets it on a plain (6:17-49). Matthew's setting on a mountain (5:1; also at 4:8; 15:29-31; 17:1-8; 28:16-20) makes Jesus a Moses-like figure, but one who exceeds Moses as authoritative Teacher of the Law. This is the first of five major discourses in the Gospel (followed by 10:1–11:1 on mission; 13:1-53 on parables; 18:1-35 on church life and order; 24:1–25:46 on the last judgment). It may have originated as a collection of the core teachings of Jesus, specifically aimed at Jewish Christians, helping them relate their new faith to their Jewish heritage. The emphasis on fulfillment of the Law and the prophets (5:17; 7:12) encircles the whole.

Several ways of outlining the structure of the sermon are possible. The Beatitudes (5:1-12) and parabolic sayings about publicly living and proclaiming them (5:13-16) lead off. Then follow six antithetical statements about the rigorous demands of discipleship (5:17-48). Jesus' interpretation of the Law is more stringent than that of the scribes and Pharisees (5:20). Next are teachings about various attitudes and actions incumbent on disciples (6:1–7:12). A highlight in this section is the Our Father (6:9-15). Rounding out the sermon are concluding exhortations and warnings (7:13-28).

5:1-12 The Beatitudes

The summary statement in 4:23-25 has brought on stage a great multitude who have been healed by Jesus and have heard his teaching. This crowd, along with Jesus' disciples, are now the recipients of detailed instruction. Throughout the Gospel the crowds are generally favorable to Jesus, but at the passion narrative they become adversarial (27:20-26).

for they will see God.
⁹Blessed are the peacemakers,
for they will be called children of God.
¹⁰Blessed are they who are persecuted for the sake of righteousness,

for theirs is the kingdom of heaven.
¹¹Blessed are you when they insult you and persecute you and utter every kind of evil against you [falsely] because of me. ¹²Rejoice and be glad, for your reward will be great in heaven. Thus they

---

Jesus assumes a sitting position, typical of teachers (5:1; Ezek 8:1) and of rulers (Matt 27:19).

The Beatitudes have echoes in Wisdom literature and the prophets (e.g., Prov 3:13; 28:14; Sir 25:7-9; 48:1-11; Isa 30:18; 32:20). Matthew casts them in eight parallel statements of blessing and promise in the third person plural (vv. 3-10) and concludes with a ninth beatitude in the second person plural (v. 11). Luke structures them into four blessings followed by four "woes" (6:20-26). Matthew relegates the woes to an extended denunciation of the scribes and Pharisees in 23:13-23. The rewards assured to disciples are already experienced to a degree in the present time ("Blessed *are . . .*"; emphasis added) but await fulfillment at the end time.

In the first blessing (v. 3), *ptōchos* denotes "beggar," that is, one who is destitute. The theme of God's care for the poor is found abundantly in the Old Testament (e.g., Exod 22:25-27; Deut 15:7-11; Isa 61:1). That wealth is an obstacle to discipleship surfaces again in Jesus' teaching at 19:16-30. Matthew's addition of "in spirit" (cf. Luke 6:20) likely reflects the struggle of those in the community with greater material wealth to live as disciples. The assurance of the "kingdom of heaven" frames the Beatitudes (vv. 3, 10).

The second beatitude (v. 4) speaks of comfort to those who mourn. This recalls the comfort Isaiah gives to Zion when mourning the destruction of the temple (Isa 61:1-3). It also points forward to the women who perform the rites of mourning for Jesus surrounding his death (26:6-13; 27:55-56, 61; 28:1-10) and the joy they experience in encountering him once again alive (28:8).

The third beatitude, "Blessed are the meek" (v. 5), does not teach disciples to be shrinking violets; rather, the word *praeis* connotes those who are not overly impressed by their own self-importance—in other words, those who are appropriately humble and considerate. This beatitude echoes Psalm 37:11, where the Hebrew word for meek, *ʿanāwîm*, is essentially equivalent to "poor in spirit." The promise of land has an echo in

persecuted the prophets who were before you.

The Similes of Salt and Light. ◄ ¹³"You are the salt of the earth. But if salt loses its taste, with what can it be seasoned? It is no longer good for anything but to be thrown out and trampled underfoot. ¹⁴You are the light of the world. A city set on a mountain cannot be hidden. ¹⁵Nor do they light a lamp and then put it under a bushel basket; it is set on a lampstand, where it gives light to all in the house. ¹⁶Just so, your light ► must shine before others, that they may see your good deeds and glorify your heavenly Father.

---

1 Enoch 5:7, where the eschatological promise refers not only to Israel but to the whole earth.

In the fourth beatitude there is an allusion to Psalm 107:5, 8-9, in which God satisfies those who hunger and thirst. Matthew adds one of his key terms, "righteousness" (see also 1:19; 3:15; 6:33), that is, right relation with God, self, others, and all creation. Disciples are to seek it actively, "hunger and thirst" for it (v. 6), through faithfulness to the demands of the covenant (5:17-20). However, there is a sober warning in the eighth beatitude that they will be persecuted for the sake of righteousness (v. 10).

The fifth beatitude assures those who exercise mercy that the same will be shown to them (v. 7). A similar assertion is made about forgiveness in the prayer Jesus teaches his disciples (6:12; see also 18:23-35). Twice in conflictual situations Jesus admonishes his opponents to learn the meaning of mercy (9:13; 12:7). At 23:23 Jesus lists mercy, along with judgment and fidelity, as the weightier matters of the Law.

In Psalm 24:4, a hymn for processing into the temple, the "clean of hand and pure of heart" are those who are not idolaters and who have not sworn falsely. They are the ones who are able to stand in the holy place and receive blessings and justice from God. In the sixth beatitude (v. 8) the promise of "seeing God" refers not to encountering God in the temple in Jerusalem (as in Pss 11:7; 17:15; 27:4; 42:3), but is an eschatological promise to be in God's presence face to face (cf. Exod 3:6; 19:21; 33:20, 23, reflecting the belief that human beings could not see God and live).

The seventh beatitude (v. 9) assures those who devote themselves to peacemaking that they will be sons and daughters of God. As Jesus has been shown to be Son of God (1:1; 2:15; 3:17), so too disciples who learn his ways of forgiveness and reconciliation share in the same intimate relationship with God. Jesus gives concrete strategies for peacemaking in 5:38-48 and 18:1-35. In the ears of Jewish Christians, this beatitude would also be evocative of God's gift of *shālôm*, not just the absence of strife, but a pervasive well-being in every arena of life.

Teaching about the Law. [17]"Do not think that I have come to abolish the law or the prophets. I have come not to abolish but to fulfill. [18]Amen, I say to you, until heaven and earth pass away, not the smallest letter or the smallest part of a letter will pass from the law, until all things have taken place. [19]Therefore, whoever breaks one of the least of these commandments and teaches others to do so will be called least in the kingdom of heaven. But whoever obeys and teaches these commandments will be called greatest in

---

The eighth beatitude (v. 10) circles back to the fourth one, regarding righteousness (v. 6), and promises attainment of the reign of God, as does the first (v. 3). The kinds of persecution that Matthean Christians likely faced were economic harassment, conflicts with Jews who did not join them, struggles over the degree of accommodation to Hellenistic culture, and the like. Jesus speaks to his disciples more concretely about the kinds of persecution they may face when he first sends them out on mission (10:16-42).

The ninth beatitude (v. 11) speaks of verbal abuse that disciples suffer because of Jesus. They are to find joy in the midst of such trials through hope in a heavenly reward and from the assurance that they are being prophetic—a ministry that always entails rejection by some (v. 12; 23:29-34).

5:13-16 Salt and light

With two metaphors Jesus speaks to his followers about how they already are salt of the earth (v. 13) and light of the world (v. 14). The first word, *you*, is emphatic in both verses, contrasting Matthean Christians with their counterparts in the synagogue. Salt was a critical necessity in the ancient world (Sir 39:26). It was used for seasoning, preservation, and purifying (2 Kgs 2:19-22). It was used to ratify covenants (Num 18:29; 2 Chr 13:5) and in liturgical functions (Exod 30:35; Lev 2:13; Ezek 43:24; Ezra 6:9). To eat salt with someone signifies a bond of friendship and loyalty (Ezra 4:14; Acts 1:4). Salts in the soil are needed for its fecundity, but soil that is "nothing but sulphur and salt" is a desert wasteland (Deut 29:22; similarly Ps 107:34; Job 39:6; Jer 17:6; Zeph 2:9). Salt scattered on a conquered city symbolically reinforced its devastation (Judg 9:45).

In telling his disciples "You are the salt of the earth," Jesus can draw on any of these symbols. Disciples preserve, purify, and judge, drawing out the savor of God's love in the world. The puzzle about how salt may lose its taste is probably best answered by salt being diluted or dissolved. Coming on the heels of Jesus' exhortation to rejoice when persecuted (vv. 11-12), it is likely a warning to disciples not to let their ardor dissipate under the rigors of persecution.

the kingdom of heaven. ²⁰I tell you, unless your righteousness surpasses that of the scribes and Pharisees, you will not enter into the kingdom of heaven.

Teaching about Anger. ²¹"You have heard that it was said to your ancestors, 'You shall not kill; and whoever kills will be liable to judgment.' ²²But I say to you, whoever is angry with his brother will be liable to judgment, and whoever says to his brother, 'Raqa,' will be answerable to the Sanhedrin, and whoever says, 'You fool,' will be liable to fiery Gehenna. ²³Therefore, if you bring your gift to the altar, and there recall that your brother has anything against you, ²⁴leave your gift there at the altar, go first and be reconciled with your brother, and then come and offer your gift. ²⁵Settle with your opponent quickly while on the way to court with him. Otherwise your oppo-

---

Disciples are also "the light of the world," like a city set on a mountain that cannot be hidden (v. 14). The metaphor has a political twist, since Cicero (*Cataline* 4.6) described Rome as a "light to the whole world." It is Jesus' beatitudinal way of life that is light to the world, not the imperial domination system. Just as the city on a mountain cannot be hidden, a lamp is not lit and then immediately extinguished (v. 15). One does not waste precious fuel oil this way. Using a vessel (*modios*, literally, a "bushel basket") to put out the light would prevent dangerous sparks from spreading.

These two images speak of the all-encompassing nature of the witness of disciples: as salt and light they influence the whole world. These metaphors also show that the disciples do not draw attention to themselves. Just as salt is most effective when it is not noticed in well-seasoned food and a lamp serves to illumine the other objects in the room, so the effect of disciples' good works is to point to God, who is glorified. In verse 16 Matthew gives the first of many references to God as "Father." See remarks at 6:9-16.

5:17-20 The Law and righteousness

These verses clearly set forth Jesus' relationship to the Law. He is a thoroughly observant Jew who is devoted to keeping the Law. He does not replace the Law, nor does he break it; rather, he fulfills it, bringing it to its intended purpose. He is authentic interpreter of the Law for a changed situation.

5:21-26 On anger

This is the first of six antithetical statements (5:21-48), each of which begins with "You have heard that it was said . . . ," followed by a command introduced with the formula "But I say to you . . ." In each instance Jesus declares a former understanding of the Law inadequate as he places more stringent demands on his disciples. Each of the six examples

nent will hand you over to the judge, and the judge will hand you over to the guard, and you will be thrown into prison. ²⁶Amen, I say to you, you will not be released until you have paid the last penny.

Teaching about Adultery. ²⁷"You have heard that it was said, 'You shall not commit adultery.' ²⁸But I say to you, everyone who looks at a woman with lust has already committed adultery with her in his heart. ²⁹If your right eye causes you to sin, tear it out and throw it away. It is better for you to lose one of your members than to have your whole body thrown into Gehenna. ³⁰And if

addresses an aspect of right relation among people in a covenantal faith community. The word *adelphos* in verse 22 refers not only to blood relations but to a Christian "brother or sister."

Killing another person is the epitome of broken relationships. The Law given to Moses forbids killing (Exod 20:13; Deut 5:18). Jesus' command is to defuse anger and work toward reconciliation before the rupture in the relationship reaches a murderous stage. He gives three concrete examples. The first is to avoid insulting one another. *Rēqā'* is an Aramaic word meaning approximately the same thing as *morē* in Greek, which is "you fool" (v. 22). Second, liturgical sacrifices do not cover over broken relationships. One must attempt face-to-face reconciliation before making ritual offerings (vv. 23-24; see similar injunctions in Isa 1; Prov 15:8; 21:3, 27; Sir 34:21-27; 35:1-4). The third example warns against letting conflicts escalate to the point of litigation in court (vv. 25-26). For disciples, it is imperative to defuse anger and attempt reconciliation, so that no conflict becomes murderous. One who lets anger simmer and grow will face judgment (v. 22) before God.

The Sanhedrin, Gehenna, and prison are all ways of speaking about judgment. The Sanhedrin was the highest Jewish judicial council (see 26:57-68). Gehenna comes from the Hebrew *gê hinnōm*, "Hinnom valley," which runs south-southwest of Jerusalem. It came to represent the place of fiery judgment, because there the fires of the Molech cult burned, and later, smoldering refuse. Prison was not used to hold debtors or other offenders long term, as verse 26 implies. Once guilt was determined, one would be executed, deported, or sold into slavery. The point is that the consequences for not working at reconciliation are dire. It is not enough for Jesus' disciples to avoid killing; they must actively seek to defuse anger and pursue right relation with all. Here Jesus is not addressing righteous anger, that is, outrage at injustice that gives energy to work toward change.

5:27-30 On adultery

Just as anger is prohibited (vv. 21-26) as the first step toward murder, so the lustful look is condemned as the prelude to adultery. The Law forbids

your right hand causes you to sin, cut it off and throw it away. It is better for you to lose one of your members than to have your whole body go into Gehenna.

Teaching about Divorce. [31]"It was also said, 'Whoever divorces his wife must give her a bill of divorce.' [32]But I say to you, whoever divorces his wife (unless the marriage is unlawful) causes her to commit adultery, and whoever marries a divorced woman commits adultery.

Teaching about Oaths. [33]"Again you have heard that it was said to your ancestors, 'Do not take a false oath, but make good to the Lord all that you vow.' [34]But I say to you, do not swear at all; not by heaven, for it is God's throne;

---

not only adultery (Exod 20:14; Deut 5:18) but also covetousness (Exod 20:17) of another person's spouse and of their possessions. Vivid metaphors of tearing out one's eye and cutting off a hand convey the seriousness of the sin of lust. On Gehenna, see verse 22.

5:31-32 On divorce

The third example builds on the previous one, adding that divorce is also a form of adultery. It is addressed to males and reflects the Jewish custom that only they could initiate divorce. The process for doing so is found in Deuteronomy 24:1. A fuller elaboration of Jesus' teaching on divorce is found in Matthew 19:1-12. Here the reasoning is not given, simply the prohibition, along with the exception for *porneia* (v. 32). Scholars are divided over whether this word connotes sexual misconduct, that is, adultery, or whether it refers to marriage to close kin, which was forbidden in Jewish law (Lev 18:6-18; see also Acts 15:20, 29).

5:33-37 On taking oaths

Now the focus shifts to address honesty in relationships. Whereas Leviticus 19:12 admonished, "You shall not swear falsely by my name, thus profaning the name of your God," Jesus insists that relations among Christians be so transparent as to end the need for taking oaths at all. Just as Matthew uses *the reign of heaven*, avoiding the use of "God" (see comments at 3:2), so here he employs "heaven" (v. 34), "earth" (see Ps 24:1), and "Jerusalem" (v. 35) as euphemisms for God. Verse 36 makes an ironic reference to coloring one's hair, a practice already used in antiquity. Christian integrity must be such that there is no need to swear in order to make another believe the veracity of their word.

5:38-42 On nonretaliation

The fifth unit concerns the *ius talionis* (Lev 24:20), which was based on the principle of equal reciprocity. The Law placed limits on retribution, so

³⁵nor by the earth, for it is his footstool; nor by Jerusalem, for it is the city of the great King. ³⁶Do not swear by your head, for you cannot make a single hair white or black. ³⁷Let your 'Yes' mean 'Yes,' and your 'No' mean 'No.' Anything more is from the evil one.

Teaching about Retaliation. ³⁸"You have heard that it was said, 'An eye for an eye and a tooth for a tooth.' ³⁹But I say to you, offer no resistance to one who is evil. When someone strikes you on [your] right cheek, turn the other one to him as well. ⁴⁰If anyone wants to go to law with you over your tunic, hand him your cloak as well. ⁴¹Should anyone press you into service for one mile, go with him for two miles. ⁴²Give to the one who asks of you, and do not turn your back on one who wants to borrow.

---

as to curtail escalating cycles of vengeance. As in the previous four examples, Jesus demands more, thus going to the core of the attitudes and actions necessary to adequately fulfill what the Law intends. The principle is articulated in verse 39a, and four concrete examples follow in verses 39b-42. Verse 39a is best translated "do not retaliate against the evildoer." The verb *antistēnai* most often carries the connotation "resist violently" or "armed resistance in military encounters" (e.g., Eph 6:13).

A command not to resist evil makes little sense on the lips of Jesus, when the whole Gospel shows him doing just the opposite. The issue here is *how* the disciple is to confront evil. The examples that follow show how nonretaliation is a strategy that breaks cycles of violence in confrontations between persons of unequal power and status. In the first three the person addressed is a victim of an injustice inflicted by a more powerful person. Retaliation by the injured party is not a realistic option. The expected response is submission. There is an alternate way to respond by actively confronting the injustice with a positive and provocative act that can break the cycle of violence and begin a different one in which gestures of reconciliation can be reciprocated.

The first example (v. 39b) involves a backhanded slap (only the right hand would be used for striking another), meant to insult and humiliate. Turning the other cheek is a creative response that robs the aggressor of the power to humiliate and shames the one who intended to inflict shame. It interrupts the cycle of violence, which is the first step toward restoration of right relation. It could begin to move the aggressor toward repentance, leading to reconciliation.

In a similar way, a debtor who stands naked in court, after handing over both under and outer garments to a creditor (v. 40), performs a shocking act that places shame on the creditor. See Genesis 9:20-27, which

Love of Enemies. [43]"You have heard that it was said, 'You shall love your neighbor and hate your enemy.' [44]But I say to you, love your enemies, and pray for those who persecute you, [45]that you may be children of your heavenly Father, for he makes his sun rise on the bad and the good, and causes rain to fall on the just and the unjust. [46]For if you love those who love you, what recompense will you have? Do not the tax collectors do the same? [47]And if you greet your brothers only, what is unusual about that? Do not the pagans do the same? [48]So be perfect, just as your heavenly Father is perfect.

---

asserts that it is the one who views another's nakedness who is shamed. Isaiah (20:1-6) made use of this strategy. This tactic exposes the injustice of the economic system to which the creditor subscribes and opens the possibility that he may repent, perceiving the common humanity that unites him with those he had exploited.

The third illustration (v. 41) envisions a situation in which a Roman soldier compels one of the subject people to carry his pack. Seizing the initiative, the subjugated person can destabilize the situation, creating a dilemma for the soldier, who worries that he would face punishment for exacting service for excessive distances.

The last example (v. 42) is addressed to the person in a superior economic position. In context it implies a situation in which there is indebtedness due to some injustice. Nonretaliation on the part of the lender would be foregoing the demand that the money or goods be returned.

Each of these illustrations gives an example of how to restore justice by interrupting cycles of violence and enmity and initiating new cycles of generosity that invite reciprocity. In this way the intent of the Law is fulfilled.

5:43-48 Love your enemy

The sixth and last in the series of antitheses deals with the command to love the neighbor (Lev 19:18). Love, as a commandment, concerns not feelings but deeds that reflect faithfulness to the covenant. Nowhere in the Scriptures is there a command to hate the enemy. It was generally understood, however, that Israelites were obliged to practice deeds of covenant fidelity toward one another, but such was not required toward those outside the covenant community. "Hate," *miseō*, not only denotes active hostility but also connotes "love less" (as Matt 6:24). For Jesus this is an inadequate interpretation of the Law. He requires the same treatment for both those inside and outside the covenant community. Concrete ways to love enemies include praying for persecutors (v. 44) and welcoming outsiders (v. 47).

6 **Teaching about Almsgiving.** [1]"[But] take care not to perform righteous deeds in order that people may see them; otherwise, you will have no recompense from your heavenly Father. [2]When you give alms, do not blow a trumpet before you, as the hypocrites do in the synagogues and in the streets to win the praise of others. Amen, I say to you, they have received their reward. [3]But when you give alms, do not let your left hand know what your right is doing, [4]so that your almsgiving may be secret. And your Father who sees in secret will repay you.

Teaching about Prayer. [5]"When you pray, do not be like the hypocrites, who love to stand and pray in the

---

"Persecut[ors]" likely refers to fellow Jews who opposed Christian missionaries, as in 10:23; 23:34. The verb *aspazomai*, "greet," in verse 47 connotes welcome and a wish for well-being, not simply a salutation.

While in previous examples the motive was to avoid punishment (vv. 21-26, 29, 30), the reason given for loving enemies (vv. 45-48) is that God acts this way, treating both the just and the unjust with the same gratuitous bounty (v. 45). Giving loving treatment only to one's own people does not adequately fulfill the Law. Verse 48 sums up: "There must be no limits to your goodness, as your heavenly Father's goodness knows no bounds" (cf. NAB: "So be perfect, just as your heavenly Father is perfect"). The word *teleios*, usually translated "perfect," connotes not so much moral perfection as completeness, full maturity, as the Hebrew *tāmîm* does (Deut 18:13).

6:1-18 Almsgiving, prayer, and fasting

There is a shift now away from the antithetical structure of 5:21-48 as this next section addresses three practices that are pillars of Jewish spirituality: almsgiving (vv. 2-4), prayer (vv. 5-15), and fasting (vv. 16-18). All the material, except the Lord's Prayer (vv. 9-13), which stands at the center, is unique to Matthew. Verse 1 sounds the theme and ties this section to the previous one. As recipients of God's limitless graciousness and mercy (5:43-48), disciples are to respond in kind, with generous deeds of righteousness (see 3:15; 5:6, 10, 20) that express and establish right relation. The emphasis in each instance is on the interior disposition. The thread of "who sees" (vv. 1, 4, 5, 6, 16, 18) and the theme of reward (vv. 1, 2, 4, 5, 6, 16, 18) run throughout the section.

6:2-4 On almsgiving

Care for the poor is frequently enjoined in the Scriptures (e.g., Deut 24:19-22; Isa 58:6-8; Prov 25:21; Sir 3:30). In performing deeds of mercy, disciples are not to call attention to themselves. The exaggerated metaphors

synagogues and on street corners so that others may see them. Amen, I say to you, they have received their reward. [6]But when you pray, go to your inner room, close the door, and pray to your Father in secret. And your Father who sees in secret will repay you. [7]In praying, do not babble like the pagans, who think that they will be heard because of their many words. [8]Do not be like them. Your Father knows what you need before you ask him.

The Lord's Prayer. [9]"This is how you are to pray:

Our Father in heaven,
hallowed be your name,
[10]your kingdom come,
your will be done,
on earth as in heaven.
[11]Give us today our daily bread;
[12]and forgive us our debts,
as we forgive our debtors;
[13]and do not subject us to the final test,
but deliver us from the evil one.

[14]If you forgive others their transgressions, your heavenly Father will forgive you. [15]But if you do not forgive others, neither will your Father forgive your transgressions.

Teaching about Fasting. [16]"When you fast, do not look gloomy like the hypocrites. They neglect their appear-

---

"blow a trumpet before you" (v. 2) and "do not let your left hand know what your right is doing" (v. 3) underscore the point that almsgiving should be done in an unobtrusive manner. Ostentatious givers already receive the reward of praise from others (v. 2). But such displays further shame the recipient, thus preventing right relation from becoming a present reality. Jesus contrasts the desired behavior of his disciples with that of hypocrites. *Hypocritēs* is the term for an actor who dons a mask (see Jesus' accusation of the Pharisees as hypocrites in 23:13, 15, 23, 25, 27, 29). It is aptly used here for those who pose as something they are not. The polemic between Matthew's community and the synagogue surfaces again at verses 2 and 5. Hypocrites are found in every religious group, and Christians are no exception. Staying centered on God is the key, as the next section on prayer elaborates.

6:5-15 On prayer

Jesus continues his denunciation of ostentatious shows of pious practices. It is not a critique of praying in a standing position, which was the normal prayer stance both for Jews and early Christians. Nor is Jesus advocating private prayer over communal. In fact, he teaches his disciples a communal prayer to *our* Father (v. 9). As in verse 2, the problematic aspect is the showiness of prayers done to attract the attention of others. Such behavior makes prayer impossible. The purpose of prayer is communication with God, for which one needs to shut out other concerns ("close the door," v. 6) and reach into the depths of spirit ("go to your inner room," v.

ance, so that they may appear to others to be fasting. Amen, I say to you, they have received their reward. [17]But when you fast, anoint your head and wash your face, [18]so that you may not appear to others to be fasting, except to your Father who is hidden. And your Father who sees what is hidden will repay you.

Treasure in Heaven. [19]"Do not store up for yourselves treasures on earth, where moth and decay destroy, and thieves break in and steal. [20]But store up treasures in heaven, where neither moth nor decay destroys, nor thieves break in and steal. [21]For where your treasure is, there also will your heart be.

The Light of the Body. [22]"The lamp of the body is the eye. If your eye is sound, your whole body will be filled with light; [23]but if your eye is bad, your

---

6). The reward is deeper communion with God (v. 6) rather than empty praise of human admirers (v. 5).

Furthermore, prayer is not a one-way street, nor does it require multiple words. Matthew stereotypes the prayer of pagans as babbling and criticizes them for thinking that they can manipulate God by deluging God with voluminous words. Jesus emphasizes that God already knows the needs of those who pray and implies that God stands ready to meet those needs (v. 8). Moreover, prayer of petition is only one kind of prayer. Jesus exemplifies prayer that flows from God's gracious initiative and responds in deeds of right relation (14:23; 19:13; 26:36-46). Jesus then teaches his disciples how to pray (vv. 9-13; see also 18:19; 24:20).

As in the rest of this section, the emphasis is on the interior disposition, "how" to pray (v. 9), not the words that are to be used. Luke 11:2-4 has a shorter version. Each evangelist tailors the prayer to his community's needs. The address "Our Father in heaven" is common in Jewish prayers. The pronoun "our" stresses the communal dimension of faith and the oneness of all children of God across all boundaries of difference. Calling God "Father" was not unique to Jesus; there are texts from the Hebrew Scriptures, Qumran, Philo, Josephus, and rabbinic literature in which this metaphor is used of God. Although it is the most frequently used metaphor (fifty-three times) by the Matthean Jesus, it is not the only one. See, for example, 13:33, where Matthew speaks of God as a bakerwoman, or 23:37, where Jesus applies to himself the metaphor used of God in Psalm 91, namely, that of a bird that gathers her fledglings under her wings. For the early Christians, "Father" expressed not so much intimacy as God's power and providence. By addressing God as "Father," they challenged the emperor's claim to be "father of the nation," asserting that only God is the supreme power.

whole body will be in darkness. And if the light in you is darkness, how great will the darkness be.

◄ **God and Money.** 24"No one can serve two masters. He will either hate one and love the other, or be devoted to one and despise the other. You cannot serve God and mammon.

◄ **Dependence on God.** 25"Therefore I tell you, do not worry about your life, what you will eat [or drink], or about your body, what you will wear. Is not life more than food and the body more ◄ than clothing? 26Look at the birds in the sky; they do not sow or reap, they gather nothing into barns, yet your heavenly Father feeds them. Are not you more important than they? 27Can any of you by worrying add a single moment to your life-span? 28Why are you anxious about clothes? Learn from the way the wild flowers grow. They do not work or spin. 29But I tell you that not even Solomon in all his splendor was clothed like one of them. 30If God so clothes the grass of the field, which grows today and is thrown into the oven tomorrow, will he not much more

The first three petitions (vv. 9-10) focus on God and are essentially reiterations of one desire, expressed in three ways. "Hallowed be your name" echoes Leviticus 22:32; Deuteronomy 32:51; Isaiah 8:13; 29:23; and is similar to a line from the Jewish *Kaddish* prayer: "May thy great name be magnified and hallowed." God's name is hallowed when people recognize and give praise for divine saving deeds (Isa 29:23) and when they keep God's commands (Lev 22:32). The reign of God is already inaugurated (3:2; 4:17); disciples pray for God to bring it to eschatological fulfillment, according to God's will for salvation and well-being for all realms of creation, "on earth as in heaven" (see 7:21 on God's will).

The remaining petitions (vv. 11-13) ask for divine assistance in satisfying human needs for sustenance, forgiveness, strength in the final testing, and deliverance from evil. "Bread" refers to both spiritual nourishment (e.g., Wisdom's banquet, Prov 9:1-6) and physical nourishment. The meaning of *epiousios*, "daily" or "for the coming day," is ambiguous. It may refer to the food one needs to survive each day, or it may allude to the eschatological Day of the Lord. The prayer recalls God's providing of manna to the Israelites (Exod 16:12-35) and cultivates in disciples this same kind of trust. There are also eucharistic overtones for Christians.

Matthew's keen interest in forgiveness and reconciliation (5:38-48; 18:1-35) is reflected in his expansion of the petition for forgiveness (vv. 12, 14-15). He draws a clear link between one's ability to forgive others and one's ability to be forgiven by God. The two flow from and into each other. Divine forgiveness comes first (18:23-35). After receiving unearned forgiveness from God, disciples are obliged to offer forgiveness to others.

provide for you, O you of little faith? ³¹So do not worry and say, 'What are we to eat?' or 'What are we to drink?' or 'What are we to wear?' ³²All these things the pagans seek. Your heavenly Father knows that you need them all. ³³But seek first the kingdom [of God] and his righteousness, and all these things will be given you besides. ³⁴Do not worry about tomorrow; tomorrow will take care of itself. Sufficient for a day is its own evil.

7 Judging Others. ¹"Stop judging, that you may not be judged. ²For as you judge, so will you be judged, and the measure with which you measure will be measured out to you. ³Why do you notice the splinter in your brother's

---

And when disciples forgive others, they are forgiven by God (6:14-15; 18:35). Matthew uses the term *opheilēmata*, "debts," (cf. *hamartias*, "sins," in Luke 11:4), a term that reminds disciples that offenses against others include monetary inequities from systemic injustices. See Deuteronomy 15 for prescriptions for relaxation of debts in the sabbatical year.

The final petition (v. 13) is for God's protection and deliverance both now and at the end time. Until God's purposes are completely accomplished, evil will still exist, ever testing the disciple to be faithful. The language of testing *(peirasmos)* is used not in the sense of God sadistically toying with people, looking for ways to determine their fidelity, but rather it acknowledges the struggle against evil in which disciples engage (as did Jesus, 4:1-11) throughout their earthly sojourn. Jesus teaches his disciples to rely on God's power and faithfulness to bring them through every trial and emerge victorious over evil (*ponēros* can be understood as "evil" or "the evil one," that is, Satan). In Matthew's apocalyptic outlook, there will be a final end-time crisis that will bring this testing to conclusion (chs. 24–25). The whole prayer has an eschatological dimension as well as a present one. Disciples rely on God's power and protection to provide for and save them for all eternity, a reality already tasted in the present.

6:16-18 On fasting

As with almsgiving and prayer (vv. 1-6), Christians who fast are not to call attention to their pious practice. The verb *aphanizō*, "neglect their appearance," literally means "disfigure" or "render unrecognizable." It may refer to covering one's head with a cloth (Jer 14:4) or with ashes (1 Macc 3:47), or neglecting to wash (v. 17). The point is that adulation is its own reward, and no further benefit will accrue to one who is ostentatious in fasting.

6:19–7:12 Ethical sayings

The next sayings are loosely connected by catchwords. Almost all of them have parallels in Luke. They make dualistic contrasts between earth

eye, but do not perceive the wooden beam in your own eye? ⁴How can you say to your brother, 'Let me remove that splinter from your eye,' while the wooden beam is in your eye? ⁵You hypocrite, remove the wooden beam from your eye first; then you will see clearly to remove the splinter from your brother's eye.

Pearls before Swine. ⁶"Do not give what is holy to dogs, or throw your pearls before swine, lest they trample them underfoot, and turn and tear you to pieces.

The Answer to Prayers. ⁷"Ask and it will be given to you; seek and you will find; knock and the door will be opened to you. ⁸For everyone who asks, receives; and the one who seeks, finds; and to the one who knocks, the door will be opened. ⁹Which one of you would hand his son a stone when he asks for a loaf of bread, ¹⁰or a snake when he asks for a fish? ¹¹If you then, who are wicked, know how to give good gifts to your children, how much more will your heavenly Father give good things to those who ask him.

---

and heaven, light and darkness, love and hate. Such clean separation does not exist in real life. What these pairs underscore is the choice disciples must make to be wholly centered on God while moving toward light, love, and heaven. The prevailing motif is trust in God's providence. The first saying (vv. 19-21) contrasts the corrosive nature of material things with the security of devotedness to God. Treasure on earth, such as clothing and linens, can be consumed by moths or insects or stolen by thieves. They also consume one's attention and one's heart. The lasting treasure is the heart centered on God, which cannot be dislodged.

In this context the saying about the eye being the lamp of the body (vv. 22-23) points out the dangers of eyeing the possessions of others, which incites covetous desire. Evil-eyed envy is one of the attitudes that is most destructive of community. Not only the individual but the whole body of believers is affected by such "darkness." The next saying (v. 24) reprises verses 19-21 with a different image. A word play makes the point all the more sharply. "Mammon," "wealth," is derived from the root ʾmn, "trust," the same root from which "amen" comes. God is the only one to whom disciples say "amen."

The last section (vv. 25-34) builds on these sayings, illustrating God's care for birds, wild flowers, and grass of the field, and assures disciples that God knows their needs and provides for them. This passage does not advocate passivity, that is, doing nothing and expecting that God will provide. Nor does it make a judgment on the faith of those whose daily reality is a desperate struggle to survive. The point is that when disciples' whole attention is centered on seeking God's reign and right relation with

The Golden Rule. ¹²"Do to others whatever you would have them do to you. This is the law and the prophets.

The Narrow Gate. ¹³"Enter through the narrow gate; for the gate is wide and the road broad that leads to destruction, and those who enter through it are many. ¹⁴How narrow the gate and constricted the road that leads to life. And those who find it are few.

False Prophets. ¹⁵"Beware of false prophets, who come to you in sheep's

---

all creation (5:6, 10, 20; 6:1), then those who have enough of life's necessities do not become obsessed with the quest for material possessions. Rather, they cooperate with God in providing for others (6:1-4), in supplying their daily bread (6:11). Likewise, those who are in desperate straits can let go of their worry. Neither obsessive anxiety about subsistence nor fixated desires on excessive accumulation have a place in the realm of God. Both are reflective of little faith (see also 8:26; 14:31; 16:8).

The present imperative "Stop judging" (7:1) not only warns about avoiding judging others but commands the listeners to desist from what they are in fact doing. As with forgiveness (6:14-15), peoples' actions redound to them in kind. It is not the case that disciples should overlook wrongdoing by another member of the community (*adelphos*, "brother," vv. 3-5). What is forbidden is hypocritical fault-finding. A wooden beam in the eye (v. 3) is a hyperbolic way of depicting an evil eye (6:23).

The saying in 7:6 is unique to Matthew and somewhat enigmatic. What is holy ("hallowed") in 6:9 is God's name. A pearl can signify the realm of God (see 13:45-46). "Dogs" is likely a reference to outsiders (see also 15:26), since Jews did not keep dogs indoors as house pets. Swine were unclean animals for Jews. So the saying is best understood as an admonition not to preach about the reign of God to Gentiles or pagans, but to concentrate the mission within Israel (similarly 10:5-6). If persecution can be expected in the mission to Israel (5:10; 10:16-36), all the more would such be anticipated with outsiders.

Verses 7-11 circle back to the theme of petitionary prayer. There is a reprise of the image of God as Father (6:9), as the sayings assure that just as human fathers provide good things to their children, so does God. The emphasis (as in 6:25-34) is on God's loving providence. Humans do not manipulate God into giving them what they want, nor does God need reminding of their needs. God does not give stones for bread (Matt 4:3; 6:11; 14:13-21; 26:26-30). When disciples seek foremost God's reign and right relation (6:33), this is readily granted. Askers receive, seekers find, and the door is opened to those who knock, even if the specific things disciples ask for are not always granted.

clothing, but underneath are ravenous wolves. ¹⁶By their fruits you will know them. Do people pick grapes from thornbushes, or figs from thistles? ¹⁷Just so, every good tree bears good fruit, and a rotten tree bears bad fruit. ¹⁸A good tree cannot bear bad fruit, nor can a rotten tree bear good fruit. ¹⁹Every tree that does not bear good fruit will be cut down and thrown into the fire. ²⁰So by their fruits you will know them.

The True Disciple. ²¹"Not everyone who says to me, 'Lord, Lord,' will enter the kingdom of heaven, but only the one who does the will of my Father in heaven. ²²Many will say to me on that day, 'Lord, Lord, did we not prophesy in your name? Did we not drive out demons in your name? Did we not do mighty deeds in your name?' ²³Then I will declare to them solemnly, 'I never knew you. Depart from me, you evildoers.'

The Two Foundations. ²⁴"Everyone who listens to these words of mine and acts on them will be like a wise man who built his house on rock. ²⁵The rain fell, the floods came, and the winds blew and buffeted the house. But it did not collapse; it had been set solidly on rock. ²⁶And everyone who listens to these words of mine but does not act on them will be like a fool who built his house on sand. ²⁷The rain fell, the floods

---

This loosely connected group of ethical sayings reaches its climax with the "golden rule" (v. 12). There are numerous parallels to this saying in both Jewish and Greco-Roman literature. In the Old Testament there are variations such as "love your neighbor as yourself" (Lev 19:18; see Matt 5:43) and "do to no one what you yourself dislike" (Tob 4:15). Admonitions about forgiveness (6:14-15) and judging (7:1-3) have already been framed in terms of getting back in kind what you do. Now this is offered as the guiding principle that sums up the whole of how disciples are to live according to the Scriptures. It closes the section that began with 5:17-20, on Jesus' fulfillment of the Law and the prophets.

7:13-29 Exhortations and warnings

The final group of sayings and parables are mostly from Q. Using dualistic contrasts, they warn about end-time consequences for doing or not doing what Jesus teaches. The notion of two ways was a common one in Judaism and early Christianity (e.g., Deut 30:15-20; Ps 1:6; Sir 15:14-17). The "narrow gate" (v. 13) and the "constricted road" (v. 14) express the difficulties involved in choosing the way of Jesus. Moreover, there are teachers or pastors ("false prophets" and "ravenous wolves," v. 15) who would lead believers astray. But it is not difficult to determine the right leaders to follow. The effects ("fruits") of their teaching and preaching easily reveal the correctness of their words (vv. 16-18, 20). The theme of bearing good

came, and the winds blew and buffeted the house. And it collapsed and was completely ruined."

²⁸When Jesus finished these words, the crowds were astonished at his teaching, ²⁹for he taught them as one having authority, and not as their scribes.

III. Ministry and Mission in Galilee

8 **The Cleansing of a Leper.** ¹When Jesus came down from the mountain, great crowds followed him. ²And then a leper approached, did him homage, and said, "Lord, if you wish, you can make me clean." ³He stretched

---

fruit is a favorite of Matthew (see references at 3:10), as is fiery destruction for one who fails to do so (vv. 19; 3:10, 12; 13:40; 18:8; 25:41).

Every major discourse in Matthew's Gospel ends with a warning to put Jesus' teaching into practice (5:2-27; 13:36-43, 47-50; 18:23-35; 24:37–25:46). This is the focus of the sayings in verses 21-23 and the parable of the two builders (vv. 24-27). Saying "Lord, Lord" (vv. 21, 22), either as a cry for help (8:2, 6, 8, 25; 9:28; 14:28, 30; 15:22, 25, 27; 17:15; 20:30, 31, 33) or as a liturgical acclamation (Rom 10:9; 1 Cor 12:3; Phil 2:11) is not sufficient; one must not only acknowledge Jesus' power but also engage it in doing deeds like his own (i.e., doing "the will of my Father in heaven" v. 21; on God's will see also 6:9-10; 12:50; 18:14; 26:39, 42, 44). The opposite is also true. Those who do mighty deeds like those of Jesus must be in intimate relationship with him, or else they risk him declaring at the end time, "I never knew you" (v. 23).

In the parable of the two builders (vv. 24-27) the point is similar. One who hears and puts Jesus' words into practice is like one who builds on a rock foundation (v. 24). This image is often used of God (e.g., Deut 32:4, 18, 31; Pss 18:2; 28:1; Isa 17:10). Now it is applied to Jesus and at 16:18 to Peter. The emphasis on hearing and doing echoes Israel's response at the giving of the Law, "All that the LORD has said, we will heed and do" (Exod 24:7; see also Deut 31:11-12). The emphasis in the parable is on Jesus as authoritative interpreter of the Law—"these words of *mine*" (vv. 24, 26; emphasis added). The conflicts with other religious leaders, both in Jesus' day and in Matthew's, lurk beneath the surface of this parable.

The Sermon on the Mount concludes with the same formula as each of Matthew's major discourses does, "When Jesus finished these words" (7:28; cf. 11:1; 13:53; 19:1; 26:1). The next major section focuses on Jesus' healing ministry.

8:1–9:38 Compassionate healing

Matthew returns to the Markan source, gathering in this section stories of Jesus healing every kind of illness. Two segments dealing with

out his hand, touched him, and said, "I will do it. Be made clean." His leprosy was cleansed immediately. ⁴Then Jesus said to him, "See that you tell no one, but go show yourself to the priest, and offer the gift that Moses prescribed; that will be proof for them."

The Healing of a Centurion's Servant. ⁵When he entered Capernaum, a centurion approached him and appealed to him, ⁶saying, "Lord, my servant is lying at home paralyzed, suffering dreadfully." ⁷He said to him, "I will come and cure him." ⁸The centurion said in reply, "Lord, I am not worthy to have you enter under my roof; only say the word and my servant will be healed. ⁹For I too am a person subject to authority,

---

discipleship punctuate these (8:18-27; 9:9-17) and prepare for the commissioning in chapter 10. The healing stories generally have the same form with the following elements: (1) the setting is described; (2) the sick person approaches Jesus and requests healing; (3) the gravity of the illness is depicted, highlighting the healing power of Jesus; (4) Jesus pronounces a word of healing and often touches the person; (5) there is a demonstration of the cure; (6) onlookers react with amazement. The healing stories focus on Jesus' power, but they do not compel people to believe. Some persons are tentative in their requests (8:2), some have great faith before Jesus heals (8:10; 9:22, 29), and others have little faith (8:26). Some reject him (8:34), and others glorify God (9:8) and preach throughout the land about him (9:31).

8:1-4 A person with leprosy

There are three healings in the initial cycle. First is a person with leprosy (vv. 1-4), who prostrates himself before Jesus (see also 2:2, 8, 11; 14:3; 15:25; 28:9). Having just instructed his disciples about doing the will of God (7:21), Jesus now enacts God's will to heal and shows that his own will is one with God's. In Leviticus 13–14 there are detailed prescriptions for dealing with leprosy (a term applied to various kinds of skin ailments, not only what is known today as Hansen's disease). Once again Jesus is intent on fulfilling the Law and sends the healed man to complete the rituals for reincorporation into the community of believers. The detail about telling no one (v. 4) is one that Matthew has preserved from Mark, but the theme of secrecy does not function in Matthew as it does in Mark. In Matthew the crowds are still with Jesus (v. 1), and Jesus' identity has been made public from the start.

8:5-13 A centurion's servant

In the second healing story, set in Capernaum (4:13; 9:1), an officer of the Roman army in charge of one hundred soldiers approaches Jesus, ap-

with soldiers subject to me. And I say to one, 'Go,' and he goes; and to another, 'Come here,' and he comes; and to my slave, 'Do this,' and he does it." ◄ ¹⁰When Jesus heard this, he was amazed and said to those following him, "Amen, I say to you, in no one in ◄ Israel have I found such faith. ¹¹I say to you, many will come from the east and the west, and will recline with Abraham, Isaac, and Jacob at the banquet in the kingdom of heaven, ¹²but the children of the kingdom will be driven out into the outer darkness, where there will be wailing and grinding of teeth." ¹³And Jesus said to the centurion, "You may go; as you have believed, let it be done for you." And at that very hour [his] servant was healed.

The Cure of Peter's Mother-in-Law. ¹⁴Jesus entered the house of Peter, and saw his mother-in-law lying in bed

---

pealing on behalf of his servant (*pais* could also mean "child"). Unlike the episode with the Canaanite woman (15:21-28), Jesus does not rebuff this Gentile. As with her (15:28), Jesus praises the faith of this non-Jew and even contrasts his great faith with that of Israel (v. 10). It is a foreshadowing of the inclusion of Gentiles from all corners of the earth (see Isa 2:2-4; Mic 4:1-4; Zech 8:20-23). Reclining with Israel's ancestors at the eschatological banquet (v. 11) is a frequently used image for the joys of the life that lies beyond (22:1-14; Isa 25:6). Matthew uses his favorite image of "outer darkness, where there will be wailing and grinding of teeth" (vv. 12, cf. 13:42, 50; 22:13; 24:51; 25:30) to contrast the fate of those for whom the eschatological banquet has been prepared but who do not accept Jesus. One unique element in this story is that Jesus heals at a distance and does not personally encounter the sick person. It highlights Jesus' authority (*exousia*, v. 9) but also may reflect a concern for ritual purity by not having Jesus enter a Gentile house.

8:14-15 Peter's mother-in-law

Third in the series of healing stories is the cure of Peter's mother-in-law. There are also elements of a call story. Unlike other healing stories, in which the sick person approaches Jesus, here Jesus takes the initiative. He sees her (*eiden*, v. 14), just as he sees Matthew when he calls him to be a disciple (9:9). Her response, "she rose and waited on (*diakonein*) him" (v. 15), also characterizes discipleship. The verb *diakonein* is used throughout the New Testament for a variety of ministries: table service (Acts 6:2), ministry of the word (Acts 6:4), financial ministry (Luke 8:3; Acts 11:29; 12:25), apostolic ministry (Acts 1:25). Also, in Matthew's version her service is to Jesus alone (cf. Mark 1:31, where she waits on "them"). See 27:55, where the many Galilean women who followed and ministered to Jesus

with a fever. [15]He touched her hand, the fever left her, and she rose and waited on him.

Other Healings. [16]When it was evening, they brought him many who were possessed by demons, and he drove out the spirits by a word and cured all the sick, [17]to fulfill what had been said by Isaiah the prophet:
"He took away our infirmities
and bore our diseases."

The Would-be Followers of Jesus. [18]When Jesus saw a crowd around him, he gave orders to cross to the other side. [19]A scribe approached and said to him, "Teacher, I will follow you wherever you go." [20]Jesus answered him, "Foxes have dens and birds of the sky have nests, but the Son of Man has nowhere to rest his head." [21]Another of [his] disciples said to him, "Lord, let me go first and bury my father." [22]But

keep vigil at the crucifixion. It is possible that Matthew has blended the story of this woman's healing with that of her call as a disciple. That Simon's mother-in-law may have played a significant role in the early community of disciples is likely from the fact that she is identified (though not by name), whereas other persons who are healed remain completely anonymous.

8:16-17 Summary

Matthew, like Mark, sets this first cycle of healings in one powerful day, rounding it off with a summary statement of all the other cures Jesus did. Typically, he cites Isaiah, drawing attention to how Jesus' healing ministry fulfills the Scriptures. This text (Isa 53:4) is from the Suffering Servant songs and points ahead to the Passion.

8:18-22 The rigors of discipleship

The link between healing and ministry is hinted at in the healing of Simon's mother-in-law (vv. 14-15; see also 9:31). But discipleship demands far more than an attraction to Jesus because of his mighty deeds of healing. To a scribe who wants to follow him, Jesus speaks soberly about the itinerant nature of discipleship (vv. 19-20). For other favorable references to scribes, see 13:52; 23:34. Jesus reminds those who have already become disciples that commitment to following him takes precedence over all other obligations and ties, even to family members. (See Tob 1:16-20 on the obligation to bury the dead; cf. 1 Kgs 19:20.) Jesus' homelessness recalls that of Woman Wisdom (Prov 1:20; Sir 24:7; see other parallels with Wisdom at Matt 11:16, 25-30; 23:34-39).

This is the first instance of the title "Son of Man" in the Gospel. This enigmatic expression is found only on the lips of Jesus. It occurs in contexts where Jesus speaks of his earthly ministry (9:6; 11:19; 12:8, 32; 13:37;

Jesus answered him, "Follow me, and let the dead bury their dead."

The Calming of the Storm at Sea. [23]He got into a boat and his disciples followed him. [24]Suddenly a violent storm came up on the sea, so that the boat was being swamped by waves; but he was asleep. [25]They came and woke him, saying, "Lord, save us! We are perishing!" [26]He said to them, "Why are you terrified, O you of little faith?" Then he got up, rebuked the winds and the sea, and there was great calm. [27]The men were amazed and said, "What sort of man is this, whom even the winds and the sea obey?"

The Healing of the Gadarene Demoniacs. [28]When he came to the other

---

16:13), his passion (12:40; 17:9, 12, 22; 20:18, 28; 26:2, 24, 45), and his future coming and role as judge at the end time (10:23; 13:41; 16:27, 28; 19:28; 24:27, 30, 37, 39, 44; 25:31; 26:64). The phrase *ho huios tou anthrōpou* ("son of man") is found in Daniel 7:14 and in 1 Enoch 37–71 for an end-time agent of salvation and judgment. It may reflect a Semitic expression, *ben ᵓādām* in Hebrew, or *bar ᵓěnāsh* in Aramaic, "son of humanity," designating a single member of the human species. Jesus may have used this phrase as a way of speaking of himself simply as a human being. It could be translated as "a certain person" or "someone" or, when used as a self-designation, simply "I." Whatever the provenance and original meaning of the expression, it is clearly used as a christological title in the Gospels.

8:23-27 Stormy fears

Having given orders at verse 18 to cross to the other side of the lake, Jesus now does so with his disciples in tow. These are ones who are willing to give up ties to home and family. But further difficulties lie ahead, symbolized by the "violent storm," literally, *seismos megas*, "a great earthquake" (see 24:7; 27:51; 28:2). The "earthquake" points ahead to the difficulties for disciples surrounding Jesus' passion. Initial enthusiasm for following Jesus can quickly give way to paralyzing fear for one's own life. But Jesus' power to preserve life, already demonstrated in his authority over disease, illness, and demons, now extends even to natural forces (see Pss 65:8; 89:10; 93:3-4; 107:29 for God's power over the threatening waters). The "little faith" of fearful disciples (see also 6:30; 14:31; 16:8; 17:20) gives way to amazement as they focus, not on the seemingly overwhelming obstacles, but on the person of Jesus.

8:28-34 Ministry at the margins

In the next healing story Jesus ventures out on the other side of the lake, which Matthew regards as Gentile territory. Demons and death

side, to the territory of the Gadarenes, two demoniacs who were coming from the tombs met him. They were so savage that no one could travel by that road. [29]They cried out, "What have you to do with us, Son of God? Have you come here to torment us before the appointed time?" [30]Some distance away a herd of many swine was feeding. [31]The demons pleaded with him, "If you drive us out, send us into the herd of swine." [32]And he said to them, "Go then!" They came out and entered the swine, and the whole herd rushed down the steep bank into the sea where they drowned. [33]The swineherds ran away, and when they came to the town they reported everything, including what had happened to the demoniacs. [34]Thereupon the whole town came out to meet Jesus, and when they saw him they begged him to leave their district.

9 The Healing of a Paralytic. [1]He entered a boat, made the crossing, and came into his own town. [2]And there people brought to him a paralytic lying

("tombs," v. 28) epitomize the forces of evil. Matthew has made the locale Gadara (cf. Gerasa in Mark 5:1), which is some five miles away from the sea. Despite the logistical difficulties, the image of swine (unclean animals) rushing down the steep bank to their watery demise vividly conveys the point. Jesus' power extends over all forces of evil, especially to those on the margins. The deeds expected at the end time (v. 29) are already begun in his earthly ministry. Unlike the story of the Samaritan woman who brings her whole town to believe in Jesus (John 4:39), the swineherds' report to their townspeople causes the opposite reaction (vv. 33-34). Jesus then returns to his home territory (9:1), where he receives a favorable reception (9:8).

9:1-8 Forgiveness with healing

Matthew preserves a tradition from Mark (2:1-12) that reflects the ancient belief that sickness and sin are related. In other New Testament texts (e.g., John 9:3) Jesus clearly asserts that sickness or disability is not due to any one individual person's sin. In a broader sense, sin can be thought of as the mortal condition that holds all people bound, from which only God can liberate. Thus when Jesus forgives the sin of the paralyzed man, some scribes accuse him of blasphemy. A scribe is portrayed favorably in 8:19, but for the remainder of the Gospel scribes are mainly adversaries of Jesus (7:29; 9:3; 12:38; 15:1; 16:21; 20:18; 21:15; 23:13-29; 26:57; 27:41). Blasphemy ordinarily refers to misusing the divine name (Lev 24:15-16; Num 15:30), but here it refers to Jesus arrogating to himself a power that belongs only to God. This is a charge that resurfaces when Jesus is interrogated by the high priest (26:65).

on a stretcher. When Jesus saw their faith, he said to the paralytic, "Courage, child, your sins are forgiven." ³At that, some of the scribes said to themselves, "This man is blaspheming." ⁴Jesus knew what they were thinking, and said, "Why do you harbor evil thoughts? ⁵Which is easier, to say, 'Your sins are forgiven,' or to say, 'Rise and walk'? ⁶But that you may know that the Son of Man has authority on earth to forgive sins" —he then said to the paralytic, "Rise, pick up your stretcher, and go home." ⁷He rose and went home. ⁸When the crowds saw this they were struck with awe and glorified God who had given such authority to human beings.

The Call of Matthew. ⁹As Jesus passed on from there, he saw a man named Matthew sitting at the customs post. He said to him, "Follow me." And he got up and followed him. ¹⁰While he was at table in his house, many tax collectors and sinners came and sat with Jesus and his disciples. ¹¹The Pharisees saw this and said to his disciples, "Why does your teacher eat with tax collectors and sinners?" ¹²He heard this and said, "Those who are well do not need a physician, but the sick do. ¹³Go and learn the meaning of the words, 'I

Not only does Jesus pronounce divine forgiveness, but he also reads others' thoughts (v. 4), another power that belongs only to God (Jer 11:20; Ps 7:9). This episode affirms another dimension of Jesus' power, while also heightening the conflict with Jesus' opponents. In addition, it portrays the important role of the faith community in bringing a person to wellness. It is the faith of the man's friends which Jesus sees (v. 2) and which causes him to act. Finally, it reflects a holistic approach to the person. Jesus heals both body and spirit, allowing the person to arise to a new life (*egeirein*, "rose," v. 7, the same verb used of Jesus' resurrection at 28:6). The crowd reacts (v. 8) in a manner similar to that of 7:28-29.

9:9-13 The call of Matthew

Interjected in a cycle of healing stories that began with Jesus ministering to outsiders (8:28-34) is the call of a tax collector, a marginalized Jew. Matthew has taken the story from Mark (2:13-17), where the tax collector's name is Levi. The change to the name Matthew brings forward the authoritative figure behind this Gospel, one of the Twelve (10:3). As in the call of the first disciples (4:18-22), the response is immediate and total. The remaining verses center on Jesus' close association with many marginalized people (v. 10).

Tax collectors were ostracized by observant Jews for a number of reasons. They were looked upon as collaborators with the Romans, and their work brought them into continuous contact with Gentiles. Moreover, they

desire mercy, not sacrifice.' I did not come to call the righteous but sinners."

The Question about Fasting. [14]Then the disciples of John approached him and said, "Why do we and the Pharisees fast [much], but your disciples do not fast?" [15]Jesus answered them, "Can the wedding guests mourn as long as the bridegroom is with them? The days will come when the bridegroom is taken away from them, and then they will fast. [16]No one patches an old cloak with a piece of unshrunken cloth, for its fullness pulls away from the cloak and the tear gets worse. [17]People do not put new wine into old wineskins. Otherwise the skins burst, the wine spills out, and the skins are ruined. Rather, they pour new wine into fresh wineskins, and both are preserved."

The Official's Daughter and the Woman with a Hemorrhage. [18]While he

---

had a reputation for dishonesty, as they would try to charge more than the amount prescribed (Luke 3:13). "Sinners" (v. 10) refers to Gentiles, who do not know the Law, as well as Jews who miss the mark in keeping the Law, either by immoral acts or because of their profession (tax collectors, shepherds, wool dyers, etc.). Eating with such people was particularly offensive (v. 11), since a shared meal signified intimate relationship. In addition, meals with Jesus foreshadow inclusion in the eschatological banquet (14:32-39; 22:1-14; 26:26-30). Dining with Jesus is not only a social event but also a means of healing (v. 12) and forgiveness (v. 13). Matthew adds a quotation from Hosea 6:6 (v. 13; see also 12:7), which reflects conflict between his community and other Jews about ritual purity. With this story the evangelist legitimates the presence and participation of all kinds of marginalized people in the community of Jesus' followers. Discipleship is offered to all who hunger and thirst for righteousness (5:6); those who think of themselves as already righteous find it difficult to be open to the call (v. 13).

9:14-17 Old and new

Inclusive sharing at table was not the only practice of early Christians that proved problematic. The question of why Jesus did not fast (see also 11:18-19) needed to be explained, as well as why Christians resumed the practice. Jews were obliged to fast only on the Day of Atonement (Lev 16:29; 23:27), but they also fasted in tandem with prayer (Ps 35:13), penance (2 Sam 12:13-25; 1 Kgs 21:27), mourning (2 Sam 1:12; 3:36), and divine revelation (Dan 10:3). The *Didache* (8:1; from the first half of the second century) notes that Pharisees fasted on Mondays and Thursdays (see Luke 18:12), so Christians took up the practice on Wednesdays and Fridays. While the bridegroom (a metaphor used of God, e.g., Hos 2:19; Isa 54:3-6; Jer 2:2, and

was saying these things to them, an official came forward, knelt down before him, and said, "My daughter has just died. But come, lay your hand on her, and she will live." ¹⁹Jesus rose and followed him, and so did his disciples. ²⁰A woman suffering hemorrhages for twelve years came up behind him and touched the tassel on his cloak. ²¹She said to herself, "If only I can touch his cloak, I shall be cured." ²²Jesus turned around and saw her, and said, "Courage, daughter! Your faith has saved you." And from that hour the woman was cured.

²³When Jesus arrived at the official's house and saw the flute players and the crowd who were making a commotion, ²⁴he said, "Go away! The girl is not dead but sleeping." And they ridiculed him. ²⁵When the crowd was put out, he came and took her by the hand, and the little girl arose. ²⁶And news of this spread throughout all that land.

The Healing of Two Blind Men. ²⁷And as Jesus passed on from there, two blind men followed [him], crying out, "Son of David, have pity on us!" ²⁸When he entered the house, the blind

---

used again of Jesus in Matt 25:1-13) is still present with the guests, it is not the time for fasting. "The days will come" (v. 15b) is a phrase often used to introduce an oracle of woe (Amos 7:2; Jer 38:31) and hints at the death of Jesus. It echoes Isaiah 53:8, where the Suffering Servant "was taken away." After the death of Jesus it is appropriate for his disciples to fast (see 6:16-18). Metaphors of new cloth and new wine symbolize the new way of Jesus. Yet there is no abandoning what went before. Matthew preserves from the Markan tradition the theme of the incompatibility of the old and the new but adds "and both are preserved" (v. 17).

9:18-26 Tenacious faith

A third cycle of healing stories begins with an account that weaves together the cure of a woman who had suffered from a hemorrhage for twelve years and that of a twelve-year-old girl who has died. Matthew trims away many of Mark's descriptive details (cf. Mark 5:21-43) and adds some that heighten the Jewish ambiance: flute players at the deathbed of the young girl (v. 23), as prescribed for funerals for even the poorest of Jews (*m. Ketub* 4:4); and "tassels" (v. 20) on Jesus' cloak, worn by Jews to help them remember to keep all God's commandments (Num 15:38-41).

In both stories the healing power of Jesus and the faith of the petitioners is central. The official, despite the fact that his daughter is already dead, prostrates himself before Jesus (as do other characters in 2:2-11; 8:2; 14:3; 15:25; 28:9). And even after twelve years of suffering, the woman with the hemorrhages still musters courageous faith. Jesus, like Elijah (1 Kgs 17:17-24) and Elisha (2 Kgs 4:32-37), has the power to resuscitate those who have died, an act that prefigures his own resurrection.

men approached him and Jesus said to them, "Do you believe that I can do this?" "Yes, Lord," they said to him. ²⁹Then he touched their eyes and said, "Let it be done for you according to your faith." ³⁰And their eyes were opened. Jesus warned them sternly, "See that no one knows about this." ³¹But they went out and spread word of him through all that land.

The Healing of a Mute Person. ³²As they were going out, a demoniac who could not speak was brought to him, ³³and when the demon was driven out the mute person spoke. The crowds were amazed and said, "Nothing like this has ever been seen in Israel." ³⁴But the Pharisees said, "He drives out demons by the prince of demons."

The Compassion of Jesus. ³⁵Jesus went around to all the towns and villages, teaching in their synagogues, proclaiming the gospel of the kingdom, and curing every disease and illness.

There are a number of similarities between Jesus and these two women that point ahead to his passion. Like the woman with the hemorrhage, he too suffers, bleeds, does not cry out, stays steadfast in faith, and attains salvation (the Greek word *sōzein*, v. 22, means both "healed" and "saved") by his courageous act. As the child of the ruler, at the time of her death, is surrounded by an unruly crowd, who ridicule Jesus for saying she is not dead, so Jesus, the child of God, is taunted by crowds of passersby, religious officials, and those crucified with him, for his trust in God to bring life from death (27:39-44). And as news spread throughout the land that Jesus had raised up the girl (v. 26), so the Galilean women will spread the news that Jesus has been raised (28:6-8).

9:27-31 Efficacious faith

Matthew brings the cycle of powerful healing stories to a climax as he doubles the number of men (also at 8:28; cf. Mark 5:2) who are blind (cf. Mark 10:46-52; see also Matt 20:29-34) and turns Jesus' question not only toward the ones seeking healing in the narrative but to the reader as well: "Do you believe that I can do this?" (v. 28). A disciple will need to answer this question with a strong affirmative before being able to call on that same power in mission (ch. 10). The men address Jesus with Matthew's favorite messianic title, "Son of David" (v. 27; 1:1; 12:23; 15:22; 20:30, 31; 21:9, 15). The warning not to tell anyone (v. 30) is a holdover from Mark's version; the theme of secrecy does not function in Matthew as it does in Mark (see also 8:4).

9:32-34 Healing and conflict

The final brief healing story reflects ancient belief that disability and illness were caused by demon possession (see also 8:28-34). Matthew keeps

³⁶At the sight of the crowds, his heart was moved with pity for them because they were troubled and abandoned, like sheep without a shepherd. ³⁷Then he said to his disciples, "The harvest is abundant but the laborers are few; ³⁸so ask the master of the harvest to send out laborers for his harvest."

10 **The Mission of the Twelve.** ¹Then he summoned his twelve disciples and gave them authority over unclean spirits to drive them out and to cure every disease and every illness. ²The names of the twelve apostles are these: first, Simon called Peter, and his brother Andrew; James, the son of Zebedee, and his brother John; ³Philip and Bartholomew, Thomas and Matthew the tax collector; James, the son of Alphaeus, and Thaddeus; ⁴Simon the Cananean, and Judas Iscariot who betrayed him.

---

the focus on Jesus' mission to Israel (v. 33, as also 10:6; 15: 24). The divided response to Jesus (as in 9:1-8) is a theme that keeps building. The crowds continue to react favorably to him until his passion (27:20-26), while the Pharisees take the role of prime opponents (see 3:7; 5:20; 9:11, 14).

9:35-38 Compassionate shepherd

Concluding this section is a summary statement (as 8:16-17) of Jesus' successful ministry of preaching, teaching, and healing. His focus remains on ministry to his own people (v. 35). This is one of the few times that Matthew does not make the reference to synagogues polemical. The stress is on Jesus' heartfelt compassion for his people. The image of shepherd as religious leader is a familiar one for God (Pss 23; 100; Isa 40:11) and for religious leaders (Ezek 34:8-12) and occurs twice more in the Gospel (10:6; 18:14-16). The metaphor shifts abruptly into agricultural imagery (vv. 37-38), as the image of laborers for the harvest leads into the mission discourse.

10:1-4 Called for mission

The mission discourse is the second of the five major blocks of teaching. It begins with the call and sending of the twelve disciples (vv. 1-15), followed by sober warnings about coming persecutions (vv. 16-25), reassurances about God's protection (vv. 26-33), and further sayings about repercussions, conditions, and rewards of discipleship (vv. 34-42). The central place of this discourse conveys to the reader that all discipleship has a missionary dimension to it. The number twelve is symbolic for the whole of the new Israel, recalling the twelve tribes that constituted the people of the covenant. "Disciples" (*mathētai*, v. 1) designates a wide group of followers (73 times in Matthew). The term "apostle" (*apostolos*, v. 2) means "one sent" and is used only here in the Gospel of Matthew.

The Commissioning of the Twelve. [5]Jesus sent out these twelve after instructing them thus, "Do not go into pagan territory or enter a Samaritan town. [6]Go rather to the lost sheep of the house of Israel. [7]As you go, make this proclamation: 'The kingdom of heaven is at hand.' [8]Cure the sick, raise the dead, cleanse lepers, drive out demons. Without cost you have received; without cost you are to give. [9]Do not take gold or silver or copper for your belts; [10]no sack for the journey, or a second tunic, or sandals, or walking stick. The laborer deserves his keep. [11]Whatever town or village you enter, look for a worthy person in it, and stay there until you leave. [12]As you enter a house, wish it peace. [13]If the house is worthy, let your peace come upon it; if not, let your peace return to you. [14]Whoever will not receive you or listen to your words—go outside that house or town and shake the dust from your feet. [15]Amen, I say to you, it will be more tolerable for the land of Sodom and Gomorrah on the day of judgment than for that town.

Jesus' bestowing his authority on his disciples to heal recalls Moses' imparting his spirit to the elders of Israel (Num 11:24-25). The commission to teach comes to disciples only at 28:20.

Matthew relies on Mark (3:13-19) for the list of the Twelve. There are slight variations in the names in Luke 6:12-16 and Acts 1:13. Matthew orders the names in six pairs and adds the designation "the tax collector" to Matthew (v. 3). About many of these figures little is known. Simon Peter always stands at the head and Judas Iscariot at the end. The Twelve (who appear again in 11:1; 19:28; 20:17; 26:14, 20, 47) do not play a major role in this Gospel.

10:5-15 Commissioning

The instructions given to the Twelve speak to all itinerant Christian missionaries as well as to those who receive and support them. They tell Jesus' envoys where and how to travel, how to approach people in new places, what to say and do, and how to handle rejection. For the community that offers hospitality to missionaries, they also provide a way to identify false prophets (7:15-23). Matthew is unique in stressing the mission to Israel (also 15:24). While a few episodes foreshadow a Gentile mission (2:1-12; 8:5-13, 28-33; 15:21-28), this does not become explicit until 28:16-20. Jesus himself likely understood his mission to be only for the renewal of his own people, while his followers subsequently understood it as intended for Gentiles as well.

Christian missionaries make the same proclamation as Jesus (4:17) and John the Baptist (3:2), and they perform the same healing deeds as Jesus

Coming Persecutions. ¹⁶"Behold, I am sending you like sheep in the midst of wolves; so be shrewd as serpents and simple as doves. ¹⁷But beware of people, for they will hand you over to courts and scourge you in their synagogues, ¹⁸and you will be led before governors and kings for my sake as a witness before them and the pagans. ¹⁹When they hand you over, do not worry about how you are to speak or what you are to say. You will be given at that moment what you are to say. ²⁰For it will not be you who speak but the Spirit of your Father speaking through you. ²¹Brother will hand over brother to death, and the father his child; children will rise up against parents and have them put to death. ²²You will be hated by all because of my name, but whoever endures to the end will be saved. ²³When they persecute you in one town, flee to another.

(chs. 8–9). By so doing, Christians are the human face of Christ still at work in the world, bringing hope and healing wherever there are illness, death, and manifestations of evil. Missionaries are to present themselves as completely vulnerable—without money, luggage, extra clothing, footwear, or weapons (a walking stick was often used to fend off beasts). They are not self-sufficient; rather, they are totally reliant on God's providence, demonstrated in their dependence on the hospitality of others. While missionaries deserve to be paid (v. 10; similarly 1 Cor 9:14), Jesus instructs them to minister without charge so that the poor are not excluded and so that they are able to proclaim the Gospel with integrity (v. 8b; similarly 2 Cor 11:7). The message cannot be tailored to what those who will give money want to hear. Missionaries are not to move around seeking better accommodations. They are to remain in one house, a visible sign of "God-with-us" (1:23; 28:20), offering peace (see above on 5:9) to all within. Like Jesus, missionaries face acceptance by some and rejection by others. When rejected, they are not to respond violently, but rather they symbolically shake off the vestiges of their encounter. Not to accept the bearers of the Gospel has dire consequences. For the story of Sodom and Gomorrah (v. 15), see Genesis 19.

10:16-42 The cost of missionary life

In addition to the self-imposed rigors outlined in 10:5-15, missionaries also face dangers from without (vv. 16-25). They may be "handed over" (v. 17; as is Jesus in 27:2, 18) to local councils of Jewish leaders, the Roman prefect, or the Herodian king. They may be flogged (v. 17; see 20:19; 23:34; Acts 22:19; 2 Cor 11:24-25) and hated by all (v. 22). Worst of all, members of one's own family or apostates from the Christian community ("brothers" and "sisters"; see v. 21) may denounce them to the authorities.

Amen, I say to you, you will not finish the towns of Israel before the Son of Man comes. ²⁴No disciple is above his teacher, no slave above his master. ²⁵It is enough for the disciple that he become like his teacher, for the slave that he become like his master. If they have called the master of the house Beelzebul, how much more those of his household!

Courage under Persecution. ²⁶"Therefore do not be afraid of them. Nothing is concealed that will not be revealed, nor secret that will not be known. ²⁷What I say to you in the darkness, speak in the light; what you hear whispered, proclaim on the housetops. ²⁸And do not be afraid of those who kill the body but cannot kill the soul;

In response to such perils, missionaries must first remember that they are heralds of the messianic reign of peace, when sheep and wolves can dwell together (Isa 11:6). Even so, they are not naïve about their opponents. When possible, they are to flee persecution (v. 23). When brought before the authorities, they can rely on the Spirit for the words by which they will bear witness. They are to endure "to the end" (v. 22), probably a reference to the eschatological coming of the Son of Humanity rather than to martyrdom. Regarding persecution, see above on 5:10-11. All these tribulations should come as no surprise to Christian missionaries, since they are following in the footsteps of their teacher (vv. 24-25). On Beelzebul (v. 25), see 12:22-37.

Three times Jesus reassures those he sends out not to be afraid (vv. 26, 28, 31). They are to proclaim boldly and openly, since the Gospel is meant for all; it is not esoteric teaching (vv. 26-27). Further, even if their life is taken, it is only their body *(sōma)* that is destroyed, not their soul *(psychē)*. Moreover, they are so highly prized in God's sight that God's providential care will never falter (vv. 29-31). One who publicly professes commitment to Jesus can depend on the same unwavering commitment from God through Jesus (v. 32). The only cautions are that there is one who can destroy the whole person in Gehenna (v. 28; see 5:22), and there are eschatological consequences for apostasy (v. 33).

A disparate collection of sayings (vv. 34-42) rounds out the mission discourse. These apply more widely to all disciples. In verses 34-37 Jesus returns to the topic of family divisions that result from allegiance to Jesus. Previously Jesus pronounced peacemakers blessed (5:9) and outlined concrete strategies of nonretaliation of violence (5:38-48). At his arrest he prohibits the use of a sword in his defense (26:52). Verse 34 does not contradict these but rather speaks about the effect of his mission. Jesus' purpose is not to create division, but his coming has provoked opposing

rather, be afraid of the one who can destroy both soul and body in Gehenna. ²⁹Are not two sparrows sold for a small coin? Yet not one of them falls to the ground without your Father's knowledge. ³⁰Even all the hairs of your head are counted. ³¹So do not be afraid; you are worth more than many sparrows. ³²Everyone who acknowledges me before others I will acknowledge before my heavenly Father. ³³But whoever denies me before others, I will deny before my heavenly Father.

Jesus: A Cause of Division. ³⁴"Do not think that I have come to bring peace upon the earth. I have come to bring not peace but the sword. ³⁵For I have come to set

a man 'against his father,
a daughter against her mother,

and a daughter-in-law against her
mother-in-law;
³⁶and one's enemies will be
those of his household.'

The Conditions of Discipleship. ³⁷"Whoever loves father or mother more than me is not worthy of me, and whoever loves son or daughter more than me is not worthy of me; ³⁸and whoever does not take up his cross and follow after me is not worthy of me. ³⁹Whoever finds his life will lose it, and whoever loses his life for my sake will find it.

Rewards. ⁴⁰"Whoever receives you receives me, and whoever receives me receives the one who sent me. ⁴¹Whoever receives a prophet because he is a prophet will receive a prophet's reward, and whoever receives a righteous

---

responses (see also 4:22; 8:21-22). The "sword" may be an allusion to Ezekiel 14:17, where the prophet speaks of a sword of discrimination that goes through the midst of the people, separating out those destined for destruction from those who will have mercy.

The sayings in verses 37-39 underscore the utter attachment to Jesus that is demanded of a disciple. A disciple who does not love his or her own family members and who does not recognize God's love revealed in those closest at hand will not be able to share that divine love with outsiders. But disciples, especially those called to go away from home on mission, must be willing to subordinate their attachment to what they love best—family and even their own life—for the sake of Jesus and his mission. Taking up one's cross (v. 38) does not refer to accepting suffering in general but refers specifically to the persecutions and sacrifices one endures for the sake of the mission. The paradoxical reward for such self-renunciation is finding life (v. 39).

The last sayings in the discourse shift focus to the receiving communities. Those who accept prophets, righteous ones, and "little ones" (see vv. 40-42; see also 18:6, 10, 14) among the disciples can expect to share in the grace of the one offering such gifts. On reward or punishment for offering a drink, see 25:35, 42.

man because he is righteous will receive a righteous man's reward. ⁴²And whoever gives only a cup of cold water to one of these little ones to drink because he is a disciple—amen, I say to you, he will surely not lose his reward."

11 ¹When Jesus finished giving these commands to his twelve disciples, he went away from that place to teach and to preach in their towns.

IV. Opposition from Israel

The Messengers from John the Baptist. ²When John heard in prison of the works of the Messiah, he sent his disciples to him ³with this question, "Are you the one who is to come, or should we look for another?" ⁴Jesus said to them in reply, "Go and tell John what you hear and see: ⁵the blind regain their sight, the lame walk, lepers are cleansed, the deaf hear, the dead are

---

VARYING RESPONSES TO JESUS

Matt 11:1–16:12

11:1-19 Jesus and John the Baptist

Matthew concludes the second block of teaching (10:1-42) with a transitional sentence, "When Jesus finished . . ." (as in 7:28; 13:53; 19:1; 26:1). Unlike Mark (6:30), Matthew does not recount the return of the Twelve and the success of their first missionary excursion; rather, he focuses on the divided responses to Jesus' mission, which his disciples also experience. The disciples do not always understand, but they, along with the crowds, continue to follow him, while opposition from the religious leaders increases.

This section begins with John's query about Jesus' identity (vv. 2-6), followed by Jesus' testimony about John (vv. 7-11), and concludes with a parable about the rejection both experience (vv. 12-19). The sayings are mostly from Q (parallel in Luke 7:18-35). Matthew noted at 4:12 that John had been arrested, and he will recount the story of John's death at 14:1-12. John's uncertainty about whether Jesus is the "one who is to come" (v. 3) seems to be at odds with the baptismal scene (3:13-17), where John appeared to know that Jesus is the "one coming after" him and is mightier than he is (3:11). The scene in 11:2-6 functions to clarify for the reader that the healings and teaching of Jesus in the previous chapters confirm his messianic identity. The kinds of deeds listed in verse 5 echo Isaiah 35:5-6. Although there is no explicit mention of the Messiah in Isaiah 35, these promises in a postexilic context are heralds of the dawning messianic era. An alternative interpretation is that Jesus is redefining what is to be expected of the Messiah. If some are looking for a military and political

65

Field of flowers with the Sea of Galilee in the background

raised, and the poor have the good news proclaimed to them. [6]And blessed is the one who takes no offense at me."

Jesus' Testimony to John. [7]As they were going off, Jesus began to speak to the crowds about John, "What did you go out to the desert to see? A reed swayed by the wind? [8]Then what did you go out to see? Someone dressed in fine clothing? Those who wear fine clothing are in royal palaces. [9]Then why did you go out? To see a prophet? Yes, I tell you, and more than a prophet. [10]This is the one about whom it is written:

'Behold, I am sending my messenger ahead of you;
he will prepare your way before you.'

[11]Amen, I say to you, among those born of women there has been none greater than John the Baptist; yet the least in the kingdom of heaven is greater than he. [12]From the days of John the Baptist until now, the kingdom of heaven

---

leader of the Davidic line such as the *Psalms of Solomon* 17-18 describe, then Jesus corrects their mistaken expectation. It is important to remember, however, that there was a variety of messianic expectations in Jesus' day. The beatitude in verse 6 underlines the paradoxical nature of Jesus' messiahship, at which many will take offense (*skandalizomai*, literally, "be scandalized"; see also 13:21, 57; 15:12; 26:31, 33).

Verses 7-15 shift the focus to Jesus' estimation of John. John is no flighty figure who runs after every would-be messiah who blows into town; rather, he is the one who has correctly identified God's anointed. He is the expected Elijah-like prophet (v. 14; see 17:10-12), the forerunner of the messianic reign. In verse 10 Matthew combines Malachi 3:1 and Exodus 23:30 to show the fulfillment of God's promise to send a messenger (John) to prepare the way for the one who heralds God's reign (Jesus). There may be an implied contrast in verses 7-8 between John and Herod Antipas, as the latter had coins minted with the symbol of a reed at the founding of Tiberias (A.D. 19). John's Elijah-like clothing (3:4) was nothing like Herod's luxurious dress.

John is a hinge figure who both prepares the way for the new era of God's reign (v. 11) and is also part of the reign, as both he and Jesus proclaim its arrival (3:2; 4:17) and suffer violence for its sake (11:12). John's imprisonment is an example of how the reign of God suffers violence at the hands of the violent who attempt to overpower it (v. 12). "The violent" who attempt to lay waste God's rule include not only human opponents, like Herod and those of his ilk, but also the demonic forces with which Jesus contends in his exorcisms and healings. The theme of having "ears . . . to hear" (v. 15) points ahead to the parables discourse (13:9, 13-17, 43).

suffers violence, and the violent are taking it by force. [13]All the prophets and the law prophesied up to the time of John. [14]And if you are willing to accept it, he is Elijah, the one who is to come. [15]Whoever has ears ought to hear.

[16]"To what shall I compare this generation? It is like children who sit in marketplaces and call to one another, [17]'We played the flute for you, but you did not dance, we sang a dirge but you did not mourn.' [18]For John came neither eating nor drinking, and they said, 'He is possessed by a demon.' [19]The Son of Man came eating and drinking and they said, 'Look, he is a glutton and a drunkard, a friend of tax collectors and sinners.' But wisdom is vindicated by her works."

Reproaches to Unrepentant Towns. [20]Then he began to reproach the towns where most of his mighty deeds had been done, since they had not repented. [21]"Woe to you, Chorazin! Woe to you, Bethsaida! For if the mighty deeds done in your midst had been done in Tyre and Sidon, they would long ago have repented in sackcloth and ashes. [22]But I tell you, it will be more tolerable for Tyre and Sidon on the day of judgment than for you. [23]And as for you, Capernaum:

The parable in verses 11-16 likens "this generation" (a pejorative phrase, as also at 12:39-42; 16:4; 17:17; 23:36) to a group of children who stubbornly refuse to play with another group, whether it is a comic game or a tragic one. Not responding to John's "dirge" nor Jesus' "flute," they instead sit (v. 16) in judgment (see 27:19). Such was also the reception accorded to Woman Wisdom, who called out her invitation to eat and drink (Prov 1:20-21; 9:3-5). But just as Wisdom is rejected by the foolish (Prov 1:23-25; Sir 15:7-8; Wis 10:3; Bar 3:12), so too John and Jesus are rejected. The accusation "glutton and drunkard" (v. 19) alludes to Deuteronomy 21:20, where it connotes a rebellious son. Verse 19b refutes this charge: Jesus is Wisdom incarnate who is vindicated (Prov 8:8, 20) by her works. For other parallels between Jesus and Wisdom, see 8:18-22; 11:25-30; 23:34-36, 37-39.

11:20-24 Consequences of rejection

To reject Jesus' invitation carries weighty consequences. The "mighty deeds" he has done (esp. chs. 8–9) should lead to repentance with understanding that he is the "one who is to come" (11:3) and Wisdom incarnate (11:19b). Capernaum, where Jesus makes his home (4:13; 8:5; 9:1; 17:24), Chorazin, and Bethsaida are villages near the Sea of Galilee. Previously Capernaum had given Jesus a favorable reception (9:8), although after his first powerful deed done there, he already spoke of his rejection by Israel (8:10-12). It is here that Jesus first clashes with the religious leaders (9:3, 11).

'Will you be exalted to heaven?
You will go down to the netherworld.'
For if the mighty deeds done in your
midst had been done in Sodom, it
would have remained until this day.
²⁴But I tell you, it will be more tolerable
for the land of Sodom on the day of
judgment than for you."

The Praise of the Father. ²⁵At that
time Jesus said in reply, "I give praise
to you, Father, Lord of heaven and
earth, for although you have hidden
these things from the wise and the
learned you have revealed them to the
childlike. ²⁶Yes, Father, such has been
your gracious will. ²⁷All things have
been handed over to me by my Father.
No one knows the Son except the
Father, and no one knows the Father
except the Son and anyone to whom
the Son wishes to reveal him.

The Gentle Mastery of Christ.
²⁸"Come to me, all you who labor and
are burdened, and I will give you rest.
²⁹Take my yoke upon you and learn

A taunt to the king of Babylon (Isa 14:12-20) is redirected to Capernaum
(v. 23). The coastal cities Tyre and Sidon were frequently denounced by
the prophets for their corruption (Isa 23:1-12; Jer 25:22; Ezek 28:11-23). For
the story of Sodom (vv. 23-24), see Genesis 19.

11:25-30 The revealer's yoke

This prayer is akin to the *Thanksgiving Hymns* from Qumran and uses
language like that of the Fourth Gospel. It stresses the intimate relationship between Jesus and the Creator and Jesus' unique role as revealer.
These verses are not to be taken as speaking of predestination or as anti-
intellectualism; rather, they speak of how those who are vulnerable and
marginalized are the most receptive to the revelation Jesus offers. The
word *hēpioi,* "infants," (v. 25) connotes both the dependence of one who is
needy as well as the inexperience of the fledgling disciples who have welcomed Jesus' teaching and his saving deeds.

In verses 28-30 Jesus, like Woman Wisdom (Sir 51:23-30), invites those
who are oppressed by the yoke of sin, suffering, economic distress, and
hard physical labor to take upon themselves his yoke. Rather than taking
up the yoke of oppressive rulers such as Egypt (Lev 26:13) or Babylon (Isa
47:6), Israel is to take upon itself that of Yahweh (Jer 2:20). God's "yoke" is
study of and obedience to Torah (Jer 5:5). To take up Jesus' yoke is not to
reject Torah; rather, it is to live by his interpretation of it (5:17-20). The
lightness of Jesus' yoke is not a lax interpretation of the Torah—quite the
contrary (5:21-48; 10:16-23)! Accepting its more stringent demands paradoxically leads to liberation from all that oppresses. This is the opposite of
what the Pharisaic interpreters do (23:4). "Rest[ing]" connotes that all the

from me, for I am meek and humble of heart; and you will find rest for yourselves. ³⁰For my yoke is easy, and my burden light."

12 **Picking Grain on the Sabbath.** ¹At that time Jesus was going through a field of grain on the sabbath. His disciples were hungry and began to pick the heads of grain and eat them. ²When the Pharisees saw this, they said to him, "See, your disciples are doing what is unlawful to do on the sabbath." ³He said to them, "Have you not read what David did when he and his com-panions were hungry, ⁴how he went into the house of God and ate the bread of offering, which neither he nor his companions but only the priests could lawfully eat? ⁵Or have you not read in the law that on the sabbath the priests serving in the temple violate the sabbath and are innocent? ⁶I say to you, something greater than the temple is here. ⁷If you knew what this meant, 'I desire mercy, not sacrifice,' you would not have condemned these innocent men. ⁸For the Son of Man is Lord of the sabbath."

created order is in right relationship, and the believing community together delights in its goodness (as God does in Genesis 2:1-3).

12:1-14 Sabbath controversies

Two conflicts between Jesus and the Pharisees advance the theme of rejection and culminate with a death threat (v. 14). In the first conflict Jesus defends his hungry disciples for plucking heads of grain on the sabbath. Deuteronomy 23:25 allows hungry persons to take grain from a neighbor's field, but they may not use a sickle. This saves poor persons from having to beg, while at the same time guaranteeing that they will not take undo advantage of the owner of the field.

The issue in Matthew 12:1-8, however, is that the disciples are breaking the sabbath. Jesus defends his disciples' action by citing two texts of the Torah. In verses 3-4 Jesus interprets 1 Samuel 21:1-6 as an illustration of how an act of compassion to respond to a human need must take precedence over cultic observance. This is reiterated in verse 7 with a quotation from Hosea 6:6. In verse 5 Matthew makes reference to the instructions on the duties of priests described in Leviticus 24:8 and Numbers 28:9-10. Jesus does not dismiss the Law (see also 5:17), but when there are differing interpretations of the Law, it is he who is the authoritative interpreter of the Law.

The second controversy (vv. 9-14), involving a cure on the sabbath, takes place in a synagogue. The question put to Jesus in verse 10 is a trap. Jesus cleverly replies, arguing from the lesser to the greater (as also 6:25, 26, 30; 10:31). His accusers readily recognize that they would rescue a

The Man with a Withered Hand. ⁹Moving on from there, he went into their synagogue. ¹⁰And behold, there was a man there who had a withered hand. They questioned him, "Is it lawful to cure on the sabbath?" so that they might accuse him. ¹¹He said to them, "Which one of you who has a sheep that falls into a pit on the sabbath will not take hold of it and lift it out? ¹²How much more valuable a person is than a sheep. So it is lawful to do good on the sabbath." ¹³Then he said to the man, "Stretch out your hand." He stretched it out, and it was restored as sound as the other. ¹⁴But the Pharisees went out and took counsel against him to put him to death.

The Chosen Servant. ¹⁵When Jesus realized this, he withdrew from that place. Many [people] followed him, and he cured them all, ¹⁶but he warned them not to make him known. ¹⁷This was to fulfill what had been spoken through Isaiah the prophet:

¹⁸"Behold, my servant whom I have chosen,
my beloved in whom I delight;
I shall place my spirit upon him,
and he will proclaim justice to the Gentiles.
¹⁹He will not contend or cry out,
nor will anyone hear his voice in the streets.
²⁰A bruised reed he will not break,
a smoldering wick he will not quench,
until he brings justice to victory.
²¹And in his name the Gentiles will hope."

Jesus and Beelzebul. ²²Then they brought to him a demoniac who was blind and mute. He cured the mute

sheep in danger on the sabbath. How much more valuable is a person in need, Jesus advances. The point of debate is whether or not the need is life-threatening, thus warranting saving action on the sabbath, which is allowed. Again, this episode highlights Jesus' authority to interpret the Law and the deadly hostility which that claim provokes.

12:15-21 Approved by God

At the center of the controversy stories in chapter 12 is Matthew's longest fulfillment quotation, that is, the use of citations from the Old Testament to interpret what he is saying about Jesus. The main point of the citation from Isaiah 42:1-4 is to underscore Jesus' identity as the one approved of and chosen by God, even as human authorities reject him and seek to do away with him. There are echoes of God's affirmation of the beloved Son at his baptism (3:17) and transfiguration (17:5). The emphasis is not on the suffering of the servant, but on his meekness and gentleness (11:29; 21:4-5). That Jesus has the spirit of God (v. 18) prepares for the ensuing controversy in 12:22-32.

person so that he could speak and see. ²³All the crowd was astounded, and said, "Could this perhaps be the Son of David?" ²⁴But when the Pharisees heard this, they said, "This man drives out demons only by the power of Beelzebul, the prince of demons." ²⁵But he knew what they were thinking and said to them, "Every kingdom divided against itself will be laid waste, and no town or house divided against itself will stand. ²⁶And if Satan drives out Satan, he is divided against himself; how, then, will his kingdom stand? ²⁷And if I drive out demons by Beelzebul, by whom do your own people drive them out? Therefore they will be your judges. ²⁸But if it is by the Spirit of God that I drive out demons, then the kingdom of God has come upon you. ²⁹How can anyone enter a strong man's house and steal his property, unless he first ties up the strong man? Then he can plunder his house. ³⁰Whoever is not with me is against me, and who-ever does not gather with me scatters. ³¹Therefore, I say to you, every sin and blasphemy will be forgiven people, but blasphemy against the Spirit will not be forgiven. ³²And whoever speaks a word against the Son of Man will be forgiven; but whoever speaks against the holy Spirit will not be forgiven, either in this age or in the age to come.

A Tree and Its Fruits. ³³"Either declare the tree good and its fruit is good, or declare the tree rotten and its fruit is rotten, for a tree is known by its fruit. ³⁴You brood of vipers, how can you say good things when you are evil? For from the fullness of the heart the mouth speaks. ³⁵A good person brings forth good out of a store of goodness, but an evil person brings forth evil out of a store of evil. ³⁶I tell you, on the day of judgment people will render an account for every careless word they speak. ³⁷By your words you will be acquitted, and by your words you will be condemned."

12:22-37 Power from the Spirit of God

This episode begins with a healing very similar to that in 9:32-34. This time the controversy centers on the source of Jesus' power. The crowd continues to react favorably, though they are uncertain about Jesus' identity (v. 23). The religious leaders, however, continue their offensive, this time accusing Jesus of exorcising by the power of Beelzebul. The etymology of this disdainful name for Satan is uncertain. Most likely it derived from "Baal-zebub," "Lord of the Flies," a Philistine deity (2 Kgs 1:2). The impact of Jesus' reply is that since his deeds of power are destroying Satan's realm, he cannot be using Satan's power. He then turns the tables and suggests that it is his opponents who are in the grip of Satan's power (v. 27). Returning to his own defense, Jesus spells out that it is by the spirit of God that he performs exorcisms (v. 28)—clear signs of the inbreaking of God's realm. Jesus, the stronger one (see 3:11), binds up Satan (v. 29) by his deeds of power.

The Demand for a Sign. ³⁸Then some of the scribes and Pharisees said to him, "Teacher, we wish to see a sign from you." ³⁹He said to them in reply, "An evil and unfaithful generation seeks a sign, but no sign will be given it except the sign of Jonah the prophet. ⁴⁰Just as Jonah was in the belly of the whale three days and three nights, so will the Son of Man be in the heart of the earth three days and three nights. ⁴¹At the judgment, the men of Nineveh will arise with this generation and condemn it, because they repented at the preaching of Jonah; and there is something greater than Jonah here. ⁴²At the judgment the queen of the south will arise with this generation and condemn it, because she came from the ends of the earth to hear the wisdom of Solomon; and there is something greater than Solomon here.

The Return of the Unclean Spirit. ⁴³"When an unclean spirit goes out of a person it roams through arid regions searching for rest but finds none. ⁴⁴Then it says, 'I will return to my home from which I came.' But upon returning, it finds it empty, swept clean, and put in order. ⁴⁵Then it goes and brings back with itself seven other spirits more evil than itself, and they move in

A series of loosely connected sayings follows. First there is a warning that one cannot stay neutral in this power struggle (v. 30). Then follow ominous sayings about blasphemy against the Spirit (vv. 31-32). This unforgivable sin is attributing to Satan what is truly of God. This is a warning to the religious leaders. They knowingly pit themselves against God by opposing Jesus. By so doing, they close themselves off from God's boundless offer of forgiveness. It is not that God refuses to forgive, but that they have consciously refused to accept forgiveness (see 5:43-48; 18:23-35). Then Matthew uses a favorite metaphor, bearing fruit (vv. 33-37; see also 3:8, 10; 7:16-20; 13:23; 21:19), to unmask further the wickedness of the religious leaders. Their deeds, and especially their spoken opposition to Jesus, reveal their true nature.

12:38-47 An evil generation

A shift of scene brings scribes and Pharisees asking for a sign from Jesus. The many signs Jesus has already performed have not led them to faith; more of the same will likewise have no effect on those who have already chosen evil (v. 39). One final sign remains: that of Jesus' death and resurrection. But even this mighty deed will not convince everyone (27:62-63; 28:17). The theme of outsiders who respond more favorably than Israel, particularly its leaders, surfaces once again (similarly 2:1-11; 8:10-12; 11:20-24), as even Ninevites and the Queen of the South (1 Kgs 10:1-13) will participate in judging the unrepentant.

and dwell there; and the last condition of that person is worse than the first. Thus it will be with this evil generation."

The True Family of Jesus. [46]While he was still speaking to the crowds, his mother and his brothers appeared outside, wishing to speak with him. [47][Someone told him, "Your mother and your brothers are standing outside, asking to speak with you."] [48]But he said in reply to the one who told him, "Who is my mother? Who are my brothers?" [49]And stretching out his hand toward his disciples, he said, "Here are my mother and my brothers. [50]For whoever does the will of my heavenly Father is my brother, and sister, and mother."

13 **The Parable of the Sower.** [1]On that day, Jesus went out of the house and sat down by the sea. [2]Such large crowds gathered around him that he got into a boat and sat down, and

---

The saying about the roaming unclean spirit (vv. 43-45) warns that in addition to initial repentance ("swept clean," v. 44), one must become filled with Jesus, allowing him to take possession and dwell within. The religious leaders appear to have everything in order (v. 44), when in fact, they are empty within (similarly 23:27-28). In addition to renouncing evil Jesus' disciples must have a full heart (12:34) that actively seeks the realm of God and a life that produces good fruit.

12:46-50 True family

The final vignette in this section brings Jesus' mother and siblings onto the scene. Matthew does not give a motive for their wanting to speak with him. Are they for him or against him? At 10:34-39 Jesus has spoken about the family divisions that disciples face. Is that the case with his own family? This is the last mention of Jesus' family members. Those bound to Jesus in discipleship are as family to him and to one another.

13:1-53 The parables discourse

The third major block of teaching comprises seven parables, two allegorical explanations (vv. 18-23, 36-43), and a theory on Jesus' use of parables (vv. 10-17, 34-35, 51-52). These puzzling stories use figurative language to speak in everyday terms about the realm of God. Yet there is usually a twist, so that they do not simply tell how life is but challenge the hearer to convert to how life can be in God's realm. They are usually open-ended, allowing for a variety of interpretations.

13:1-9 Parable of the sower, seed, soil, harvest

The scene shifts from the controversies with religious leaders to a large crowd eager for Jesus' teaching (vv. 1-2). Matthew's rendition closely follows

the whole crowd stood along the shore. ³And he spoke to them at length in parables, saying: "A sower went out to sow. ⁴And as he sowed, some seed fell on the path, and birds came and ate it up. ⁵Some fell on rocky ground, where it had little soil. It sprang up at once because the soil was not deep, ⁶and when the sun rose it was scorched, and it withered for lack of roots. ⁷Some seed fell among thorns, and the thorns grew up and choked it. ⁸But some seed fell on rich soil, and produced fruit, a hundred or sixty or thirtyfold. ⁹Whoever has ears ought to hear."

The Purpose of Parables. ¹⁰The disciples approached him and said, "Why do you speak to them in parables?" ¹¹He said to them in reply, "Because knowledge of the mysteries of the kingdom of

that of Mark (4:1-9). A different message comes forth, depending on which "character" is the focus: the sower, the seed, the soil, or the harvest. The sower is usually thought to represent God or Jesus, while the seed is the word of God (vv. 18-23). When focusing on the sower, the central point concerns how the farmer acts: he indiscriminately sows seed on every type of ground, offering the word to everyone, regardless of their potential for accepting it (similarly 5:45). The exhortation in verse 9 recalls the *Shemaʾ*, ("Hear O Israel," Deut 6:4-5), prayed each day by observant Jews. This prayer underscores Israel's unique relationship with God, while Jesus' parable widens the invitation to all.

When the seed is the focus, the point shifts to the reliability of the seed to bring forth a yield, even though it first seems that there will be no harvest. The parable echoes Isaiah 55:10-11, assuring that God's word does accomplish its purpose, even though much of it falls on deaf ears. Shifting attention to the harvest, the point is the assurance not only that the work will eventually bear fruit but that the harvest will explode in staggering proportions. The huge amounts in verse 8 are hyperbolic and propel the hearer into an eschatological scenario. The image of harvest is often used to speak of the end time (see also 13:30, 39; 21:34, 41). A good harvest yields up to tenfold. One that produces one hundred or sixty or thirtyfold is unimaginable. Fulfillment at the end time will far exceed all that we know here and now. Finally, if one focuses on the soil, the message concerns the quality and conditions needed for the word to be nurtured and come to fruition in the lives of disciples. The explanation in verses 18-23 elaborates this interpretation.

13:10-17 The reason for speaking in parables

Matthew, in contrast to Mark (4:1-12), draws a clear division between Jesus' disciples and the crowd. Rather than ask Jesus to explain the parable

heaven has been granted to you, but to them it has not been granted. ¹²To anyone who has, more will be given and he will grow rich; from anyone who has not, even what he has will be taken away. ¹³This is why I speak to them in parables, because 'they look but do not see and hear but do not listen or understand.' ¹⁴Isaiah's prophecy is fulfilled in them, which says:

'You shall indeed hear but not
    understand
 you shall indeed look but never
    see.
¹⁵Gross is the heart of this people,
    they will hardly hear with their
    ears, they have closed
    their eyes, lest they see
    with their eyes
 and hear with their ears

and understand with their heart
    and be converted,
 and I heal them.'

The Privilege of Discipleship. ¹⁶"But blessed are your eyes, because they see, and your ears, because they hear. ¹⁷Amen, I say to you, many prophets and righteous people longed to see what you see but did not see it, and to hear what you hear but did not hear it.

The Explanation of the Parable of the Sower. ¹⁸"Hear then the parable of the sower. ¹⁹The seed sown on the path is the one who hears the word of the kingdom without understanding it, and the evil one comes and steals away what was sown in his heart. ²⁰The seed sown on rocky ground is the one who hears the word and receives it at once

---

to them, the disciples ask why Jesus speaks to the crowd in parables (v. 10). Jesus explains that disciples have been given a gift from God to understand the "mysteries of the kingdom of heaven" (v. 11), that is, the presence of God's realm in Jesus and his ministry. Verses 13-17 emphasize human responsibility to respond to God's gift. The effect of the quotation from Isaiah 6:9-10 is to place the blame for not understanding on those who deliberately block their ears to God's word, in contrast to the blessedness of those who do respond to God's grace (vv. 16-17).

13:18-23 Explanation of the parable of the soil

Rarely in the Gospels are parables explained. This and the explanation of the weeds and wheat (13:36-43) are exceptions. Ordinarily parables are open-ended, requiring the hearer to wrestle with their enigmatic challenges. Most likely 13:18-23 represents an interpretation by the early church rather than words from Jesus' lips. The allegorical explanation focuses on the varying levels of receptivity of the four different types of soil, that is, the four types of hearers of the word. The emphasis is on the hearer; each is exhorted to cull out all impediments to becoming "rich soil." The parable also helps explain why some hearers of the word "bear fruit" and others don't.

with joy. ²¹But he has no root and lasts only for a time. When some tribulation or persecution comes because of the word, he immediately falls away. ²²The seed sown among thorns is the one who hears the word, but then worldly anxiety and the lure of riches choke the word and it bears no fruit. ²³But the seed sown on rich soil is the one who hears the word and understands it, who indeed bears fruit and yields a hundred or sixty or thirtyfold."

The Parable of the Weeds among the Wheat. ²⁴He proposed another parable to them. "The kingdom of heaven may be likened to a man who sowed good seed in his field. ²⁵While everyone was asleep his enemy came and sowed weeds all through the wheat, and then went off. ²⁶When the crop grew and bore fruit, the weeds appeared as well. ²⁷The slaves of the householder came to him and said, 'Master, did you not sow good seed in your field? Where have the weeds come from?' ²⁸He answered, 'An enemy has done this.' His slaves said to him, 'Do you want us to go and pull them up?' ²⁹He replied, 'No, if you pull up the weeds you might uproot the wheat along with them. ³⁰Let them grow together until harvest; then at harvest time I will say to the harvesters,

13:24-30 Weeds among the wheat

This parable, unique to Matthew, wrestles with the questions of who is responsible for evil (vv. 27-28a) and what is to be done about it (vv. 28b-30). The first question is easily answered: an enemy is responsible (v. 28). The more difficult question is what is the best course of action to take with regard to the weeds. The householder's reply is startling, since the best method is to eradicate the weeds as early as possible. To try to separate the two at harvest is difficult and not totally effective. Moreover, to let the two grow together poses danger to the wheat seedlings as they compete for water and nutrients.

The parable does not tell whether the householder's plan succeeded. If one presumes that it did, then the parable assures that the forces of good can withstand the forces of evil, and it advocates patient trust in the One whose job it is to do the separating at the end time. Alternatively, if the householder is seen as a foolish absentee landlord who greedily thinks that even the weeds can bring him benefit as fuel, then the parable speaks of good news to peasants who watch exploitive landowners brought down by one of their own. One other twist may be that the parable invites nonretaliation against an enemy (as 5:43-48), an action that is vindicated in the end time.

13:31-32 Mischievous mustard

The most common interpretation of this parable is that just as a tiny mustard seed grows into a large tree, so the realm of God grows enormously

"First collect the weeds and tie them in bundles for burning; but gather the wheat into my barn.""

The Parable of the Mustard Seed. [31]He proposed another parable to them. "The kingdom of heaven is like a mustard seed that a person took and sowed in a field. [32]It is the smallest of all the seeds, yet when full-grown it is the largest of plants. It becomes a large bush, and the 'birds of the sky come and dwell in its branches.'"

The Parable of the Yeast. [33]He spoke to them another parable. "The kingdom of heaven is like yeast that a woman took and mixed with three measures of wheat flour until the whole batch was leavened."

The Use of Parables. [34]All these things Jesus spoke to the crowds in parables. He spoke to them only in parables, [35]to fulfill what had been said through the prophet:

"I will open my mouth in parables,

---

from its small beginnings. But this explanation misses the possible twist and the call for conversion that may lie beneath the surface. That the mustard becomes a large tree *(dendron)*, a botanical impossibility, may point to a burlesque of the image in Ezekiel 17, 31, and Daniel 4. Rather than think of the coming reign of God as a majestic cedar tree imported from Lebanon, Jesus uses the image of a lowly garden herb that grows right in one's own backyard. God's realm is not like a dominating empire, but its power erupts out of weakness. Its transformative power comes from unpretentious ventures of faith by Jesus' disciples. Moreover, the uncontrollable growth of mustard, crossing over boundaries to mix with other crops, offers an image for the manner in which Gentile Christians were growing exponentially and intermingling with Jewish believers in the Matthean community.

13:33-35 Hiding leaven

Important to the meaning of this parable is that in every other instance in Scripture in which leaven occurs, it represents evil or corruption (Exod 12:15-20, 34; Mark 8:15; Luke 12:1; 1 Cor 5:6-7; Gal 5:9). The startling message is that the reign of God is like a batch of dough that has been permeated by "corruptive" agents. It offers both hope to those who have been on the margins or excluded and a challenge to those who are in a privileged position. An odd detail is that the woman hides *(kryptō)* the leaven in the dough, which brings out again the paradox of hiddenness and revelation with regard to Jesus and his message (10:26; 11:25; 13:35, 44). It is also important to note that it is the work of a woman that is the vehicle for God's revelation. The amount of flour also indicates a revelation of God is in the offing. Every time a character in the Scriptures bakes with three measures

I will announce what has lain hidden from the foundation [of the world]."

The Explanation of the Parable of the Weeds. ³⁶Then, dismissing the crowds, he went into the house. His disciples approached him and said, "Explain to us the parable of the weeds in the field." ³⁷He said in reply, "He who sows good seed is the Son of Man, ³⁸the field is the world, the good seed the children of the kingdom. The weeds are the children of the evil one, ³⁹and the enemy who sows them is the devil. The harvest is the end of the age, and the harvesters are angels. ⁴⁰Just as weeds are collected and burned [up] with fire, so will it be at the end of the age. ⁴¹The Son of Man will send his angels, and they will collect out of his kingdom all who cause others to sin and all evildoers. ⁴²They will throw them into the fiery furnace, where there will be wailing and grinding of teeth. ⁴³Then the righteous will shine like the sun in the kingdom of their Father. Whoever has ears ought to hear.

More Parables. ⁴⁴"The kingdom of heaven is like a treasure buried in a field, which a person finds and hides again, and out of joy goes and sells all that he has and buys that field. ⁴⁵Again,

---

of flour (approximately fifty pounds!), it is in preparation for heavenly visitors (Gen 18:6; Judg 6:19; 1 Sam 1:24). In verses 34-35 Matthew quotes Psalm 78:2 to explain again (as in 13:10-17) that Jesus' disciples have a privileged place of understanding, while the message remains hidden to the crowds.

13:36-43 The weeds and wheat explained

The allegorical explanation of the parable in 13:24-30 is likely not from the lips of Jesus but represents how the early Christians made sense of it (as with 13:18-23). The audience shifts from the crowds to Jesus' disciples (v. 36), as they become privy once again to special understanding. Each detail is given a symbolic meaning. The tone is apocalyptic as evildoers are separated once and for all from the righteous and their opposite fates are sealed. A warning is sounded to anyone who will listen that they be found among the "children of the kingdom" and not among the "children of the evil one." There is a shift from 13:16, where the disciples were blessed *because* they see and hear; now the possibility lies open that a disciple may not hear (v. 43).

13:44-53 Treasure found, stored, and shared

The parables of the buried treasure (v. 44) and the pearl of great price (vv. 45-46) offer two different ways of coming upon the reign of God: finding it unexpectedly or after a diligent search. Both speak of the total response required (as also 4:18-22; 9:9). The emphasis, however, is not on

the kingdom of heaven is like a merchant searching for fine pearls. ⁴⁶When he finds a pearl of great price, he goes and sells all that he has and buys it. ⁴⁷Again, the kingdom of heaven is like a net thrown into the sea, which collects fish of every kind. ⁴⁸When it is full they haul it ashore and sit down to put what is good into buckets. What is bad they throw away. ⁴⁹Thus it will be at the end of the age. The angels will go out and separate the wicked from the righteous ⁵⁰and throw them into the fiery furnace, where there will be wailing and grinding of teeth.

Treasures New and Old. ⁵¹"Do you understand all these things?" They answered, "Yes." ⁵²And he replied, "Then every scribe who has been instructed in the kingdom of heaven is like the head of a household who brings from his storeroom both the new and the old." ⁵³When Jesus finished these parables, he went away from there.

V. Jesus, the Kingdom, and the Church

The Rejection at Nazareth. ⁵⁴He came to his native place and taught the people in their synagogue. They were

how much one has to give up, but on the immense joy that comes from the complete investment of self and resources in God's realm. The parable of the net (vv. 47-48) and its explanation (vv. 49-50) mirrors that of the weeds and the wheat and its interpretation (13:24-30, 36-43), both in wording and message.

The final verses (51-52) tie together the whole parable discourse in chapter 13. The disciples have a certain privileged level of understanding (13:11-12, 16-17), but their comprehension is by no means complete. The saying about scribes who have been instructed is often thought to be a self-portrait of the evangelist, but it actually characterizes the educated disciple, schooled in Jesus' interpretation of the Law, thus knowing how to preserve what is essential from the old for a new reality.

13:54-58 Rejected prophet

The divided responses to Jesus' teaching play out not only with disciples and crowds, as in the previous discourse on the parables, but also with his own family and neighbors. In a close-knit village, everyone presumes to know everything about Jesus, yet he startles them with his wisdom and mighty deeds. As they puzzle over the source of Jesus' power, the reader is led to supply the answer with a response of faith. The reference to Jesus' siblings has been understood in various ways: as other children of Mary and Joseph, cousins of Jesus, or Joseph's children from an earlier marriage. It is not clear whether Matthew knew the tradition about Mary's perpetual virginity (see 1:25).

astonished and said, "Where did this man get such wisdom and mighty deeds? [55]Is he not the carpenter's son? Is not his mother named Mary and his brothers James, Joseph, Simon, and Judas? [56]Are not his sisters all with us? Where did this man get all this?" [57]And they took offense at him. But Jesus said to them, "A prophet is not without honor except in his native place and in his own house." [58]And he did not work many mighty deeds there because of their lack of faith.

14 **Herod's Opinion of Jesus.** [1]At that time Herod the tetrarch heard of the reputation of Jesus [2]and said to his servants, "This man is John the Baptist. He has been raised from the dead; that is why mighty powers are at work in him."

The Death of John the Baptist. [3]Now Herod had arrested John, bound [him],

and put him in prison on account of Herodias, the wife of his brother Philip, [4]for John had said to him, "It is not lawful for you to have her." [5]Although he wanted to kill him, he feared the people, for they regarded him as a prophet. [6]But at a birthday celebration for Herod, the daughter of Herodias performed a dance before the guests and delighted Herod [7]so much that he swore to give her whatever she might ask for. [8]Prompted by her mother, she said, "Give me here on a platter the head of John the Baptist." [9]The king was distressed, but because of his oaths and the guests who were present, he ordered that it be given, [10]and he had John beheaded in the prison. [11]His head was brought in on a platter and given to the girl, who took it to her mother. [12]His disciples came and took away the corpse and buried him; and they went and told Jesus.

14:1-12 Death of John the Baptist

The theme of the rejection of Jesus by his own is heightened as Jesus' likeness to John is voiced by Herod (see also 16:14). John's arrest was the catalyst for Jesus to begin his ministry in Galilee (4:12) and to reveal himself as the coming One and Wisdom incarnate (11:2-19). Like John, Jesus too will be executed and buried by his disciples. Matthew follows Mark 6:14-29 in retelling John's death. He shortens and simplifies the account, shifting the spotlight more toward Herod, not his wife, as the responsible one.

14:13-21 Feeding of the five thousand

In contrast to Herod's deadly banquet, where the king seeks to satisfy his own desires, Jesus hosts a vast multitude, healing and feeding them until they are all satisfied (v. 20). From the midst of his own grief at the death of his mentor (v. 13), his wounded heart fills with compassion for others who are suffering (v. 14). The same faithful God who provided manna and quail for Israel in the wilderness wandering (Exod 16; Num 11:31-35) and who worked through Elisha to feed a hungry crowd (2 Kgs

The Return of the Twelve and the Feeding of the Five Thousand. ¹³When Jesus heard of it, he withdrew in a boat to a deserted place by himself. The crowds heard of this and followed him on foot from their towns. ¹⁴When he disembarked and saw the vast crowd, his heart was moved with pity for them, and he cured their sick. ¹⁵When it was evening, the disciples approached him and said, "This is a deserted place and it is already late; dismiss the crowds so that they can go to the villages and buy food for themselves." ¹⁶[Jesus] said to them, "There is no need for them to go away; give them some food yourselves." ¹⁷But they said to him, "Five loaves and two fish are all we have here." ¹⁸Then he said, "Bring them here to me," ¹⁹and he ordered the crowds to sit down on the grass. Taking the five loaves and the two fish, and looking up to heaven, he said the blessing, broke the loaves, and gave them to the disciples, who in turn gave them to the crowds. ²⁰They all ate and were satisfied, and they picked up the fragments left over—twelve wicker baskets full. ²¹Those who ate were about five thousand men, not counting women and children.

The Walking on the Water. ²²Then he made the disciples get into the boat and precede him to the other side, while he dismissed the crowds. ²³After doing so, he went up on the mountain by himself to pray. When it was evening he was there alone. ²⁴Meanwhile

4:42-44) acts now through Jesus to bring well-being to the people. Jesus' saying that many would come from east and west to eat with Israel's ancestors in the realm of God (8:11) is enacted here. The parable of the great banquet (22:1-10) will also return to this theme. The parallels with the Last Supper (26:26) are unmistakable as Jesus takes, blesses, breaks, and gives the bread. There are also overtones of the eschatological banquet envisioned by Isaiah (25:6-10). In contrast to the disciples' solution to have all in the crowd take care of themselves, Jesus points them toward the abundance—even surfeit—of resources that are already in their midst to be shared (see also 15:32-39). Matthew makes it explicit that the participants in this feast are women and children as well as men (v. 21).

14:22-36 Walking on water

This is the second time that Jesus demonstrates his mastery over the water. In 8:23-27 Jesus calmed the sea and the disciples' dread in the midst of a storm. In this episode Jesus shows himself to be like God, both in his ability to tread on the water (e.g., Ps 77:19; Job 9:8; 38:16) and in his self-identification as *egō eimi*, literally "I am" (v. 27), the self-designation of God to Moses (Exod 3:14). While in the Markan episode the disciples remain uncomprehending and resistant to this epiphany (6:45-52), Matthew

the boat, already a few miles offshore, was being tossed about by the waves, for the wind was against it. [25]During the fourth watch of the night, he came toward them, walking on the sea. [26]When the disciples saw him walking on the sea they were terrified. "It is a ghost," they said, and they cried out in fear. [27]At once [Jesus] spoke to them, "Take courage, it is I; do not be afraid." [28]Peter said to him in reply, "Lord, if it is you, command me to come to you on the water." [29]He said, "Come." Peter got out of the boat and began to walk on the water toward Jesus. [30]But when he saw how [strong] the wind was he became frightened; and, beginning to sink, he cried out, "Lord, save me!" [31]Immediately Jesus stretched out his hand and caught him, and said to him, "O you of little faith, why did you doubt?" [32]After they got into the boat, the wind died down. [33]Those who were in the boat did him homage, saying, "Truly, you are the Son of God."

The Healings at Gennesaret. [34]After making the crossing, they came to land at Gennesaret. [35]When the men of that place recognized him, they sent word to all the surrounding country. People brought to him all those who were sick [36]and begged him that they might touch only the tassel on his cloak, and as many as touched it were healed.

15 **The Tradition of the Elders.** [1]Then Pharisees and scribes came to Jesus from Jerusalem and said, [2]"Why do your disciples break the tradition of the elders? They do not wash [their] hands when they eat a meal." [3]He said to them in reply, "And why do you break the commandment of God for the sake of your tradition? [4]For God

adds a poignant vignette that captures the faltering attempts of the disciples, represented by Peter (see also 16:18-19), to overcome their fears and to step out with Jesus in faith. His power to save (1:21; 8:25) takes them beyond their little faith (also 6:30; 8:26; 16:8; 17:20) to the ability to proclaim him "Son of God" (see 3:17; 16:16; 17:5; 27:54).

Jesus continues his saving ministry to all those who are sick. As a pious Jew, he is wearing tassels as a reminder to keep God's commandments (Num 15:38-40; Deut 22:12). Those who want to touch these are expressing their desire to live in the way that is faithful to God, through Jesus (as also the woman with a hemorrhage, 9:20-22). All who do so are saved (the verb *diesōthēsan*, v. 36, means both "saved" and "healed").

15:1-20 Blind guides

This section begins with a confrontation between Jesus and the religious leaders (vv. 1-9), followed by a declaration of Jesus to the crowd (vv. 10-11), then a discussion between Jesus and his disciples (vv. 12-20). Matthew follows Mark (7:1-23) but makes substantial changes. He tones down Mark's sweeping critique of Jewish practices (7:13), although he

said, 'Honor your father and your mother,' and 'Whoever curses father or mother shall die.' ⁵But you say, 'Whoever says to father or mother, "Any support you might have had from me is dedicated to God," ⁶need not honor his father.' You have nullified the word of God for the sake of your tradition. ⁷Hypocrites, well did Isaiah prophesy about you when he said:

⁸'This people honors me with their
    lips,
  but their hearts are far from me;
⁹in vain do they worship me,
  teaching as doctrines human
    precepts.' "

¹⁰He summoned the crowd and said to them, "Hear and understand. ¹¹It is not what enters one's mouth that defiles that person; but what comes out of the mouth is what defiles one." ¹²Then his disciples approached and said to him, "Do you know that the Pharisees took offense when they heard what you said?" ¹³He said in reply, "Every plant that my heavenly Father has not planted will be uprooted. ¹⁴Let them alone; they are blind guides [of the blind]. If a blind person leads a blind person, both will fall into a pit." ¹⁵Then Peter said to him in reply, "Explain [this] parable to us." ¹⁶He said to them, "Are even you still without understanding? ¹⁷Do you not realize that everything that enters the mouth passes into the stomach and is expelled into the latrine? ¹⁸But the things that come out of the mouth come from the heart, and they defile. ¹⁹For from the heart come evil thoughts, murder,

---

does heighten the censure of the Pharisees with his addition of verses 13-14. In contrast to Mark's mostly Gentile community, Matthew's community probably still observed many of the Jewish practices and did not find these incompatible with Jesus' teaching.

The "tradition of the elders" (v. 2) refers to customs and regulations passed down orally, interpreting how to live the Law in everyday life. These began to be codified in written collections around A.D. 200. The debate over the level of authority such traditions carried was a lively one both in Jesus' day and in Matthew's. Jesus denounces those whose interpretation is not in accord with God's intent (vv. 3, 6). As examples, he cites the imposition of purity practices (v. 2), meant only for priests (Exod 30: 19; 40:12); distorted use of *korban*, the custom of declaring something dedicated to God (vv. 3-9); and giving cultic purity (regarding unclean foods) priority over moral purity (v. 11). Purity of the heart is fundamental (vv. 17-20); from this all authentic ritual practice flows.

The quotation from Isaiah 29:13 (vv. 8-9) is an invitation to the hearers to open their hearts to Jesus (similarly 13:15, 19). In contrast to Jesus, who leads the blind to sight and faith (9:27-31; 20:30-34), his opponents are blind guides (see also 23:16, 17, 19, 24, 26), taking themselves and others toward disaster and judgment.

adultery, unchastity, theft, false witness, blasphemy. ²⁰These are what defile a person, but to eat with unwashed hands does not defile."

The Canaanite Woman's Faith. ²¹Then Jesus went from that place and withdrew to the region of Tyre and Sidon. ²²And behold, a Canaanite woman of that district came and called out, "Have pity on me, Lord, Son of David! My daughter is tormented by a demon." ²³But he did not say a word in answer to her. His disciples came and asked him, "Send her away, for she keeps calling out after us." ²⁴He said in reply, "I was sent only to the lost sheep of the house of Israel." ²⁵But the woman came and did him homage, saying, "Lord, help me." ²⁶He said in reply, "It is not right to take the food of the children and throw it to the dogs." ²⁷She said, "Please, Lord, for even the dogs eat the scraps that fall from the table of their masters." ²⁸Then Jesus said to her in reply, "O woman, great is your faith! Let it be done for you as you wish." And her daughter was healed from that hour.

The Healing of Many People. ²⁹Moving on from there Jesus walked by the Sea of Galilee, went up on the

15:21-28 Tenacious faith

This is one of the most disturbing episodes in the Gospel. In no other story does Jesus ignore and then insult a person who comes to him in need. Matthew does not say why Jesus is headed toward the pagan coastal region; it is not to extend his mission beyond his own people (v. 24; see also 9:36; 10:6; 18:12). There are two tensions in this story: they involve crossing both ethnic and gender boundaries. The cry of the Canaanite woman, *eleēson me*, "Have pity on me," recalls Psalm 109:26 and the pleas of the blind men (9:27; 20:30, 31) and the father of the boy with epilepsy (17:15). This is also a liturgical formula, which may reveal tensions in Matthew's community not only over Gentile inclusion but also over the role of women in the liturgical and theological life of the community.

Jesus' retort (v. 26) may allude to Isaiah 56:10, where those who are blind and without knowledge are like "dumb dogs." Or it may allude to the tension between Galileans and coastal peoples, as the Galileans often saw their grain exported to Tyre and Sidon, leaving themselves without enough (see Acts 12:20). The woman's clever response displays her great and tenacious faith (v. 28), which contrasts with that of the disciples, whose fearfulness so often displays their "little faith" (6:30; 8:26; 14:31; 16:8; 17:20). Perhaps Jesus' confrontation with this woman was a turning point in his understanding of his mission to all peoples (28:19).

15:29-39 Healing and feeding more multitudes

This episode replays 14:15-21 with slight differences. Unlike the Markan feeding stories (6:34-44; 8:1-10), where the first takes place in

mountain, and sat down there. ³⁰Great crowds came to him, having with them the lame, the blind, the deformed, the mute, and many others. They placed them at his feet, and he cured them. ³¹The crowds were amazed when they saw the mute speaking, the deformed made whole, the lame walking, and the blind able to see, and they glorified the God of Israel.

The Feeding of the Four Thousand. ³²Jesus summoned his disciples and said, "My heart is moved with pity for the crowd, for they have been with me now for three days and have nothing to eat. I do not want to send them away hungry, for fear they may collapse on the way." ³³The disciples said to him, "Where could we ever get enough bread in this deserted place to satisfy such a crowd?" ³⁴Jesus said to them, "How many loaves do you have?" "Seven," they replied, "and a few fish." ³⁵He ordered the crowd to sit down on the ground. ³⁶Then he took the seven loaves and the fish, gave thanks, broke the loaves, and gave them to the disciples, who in turn gave them to the crowds. ³⁷They all ate and were satisfied. They picked up the fragments left over—seven baskets full. ³⁸Those who ate were four thousand men, not counting women and children. ³⁹And when he had dismissed the crowds, he got into the boat and came to the district of Magadan.

16 **The Demand for a Sign.** ¹The Pharisees and Sadducees came and, to test him, asked him to show them a sign from heaven. ²He said to

Jewish territory and the second on the Gentile side of the lake, Matthew makes no such distinction. For him, Jesus' mission is still restricted to Israel (10:5; 15:24). As in 14:15-21, the feeding is linked with healing. This time there is also a didactic element. Jesus sits on a mountaintop (v. 29), a teacher akin to Moses (see also 5:1; 17:1; 28:16). The disciples seem to have progressed in their understanding. This time they do not propose to Jesus that the crowd be sent away to find food for themselves. They are ready with seven loaves, and, as before, they help Jesus distribute them. While the same theological motifs are in play as in 14:15-21, there is slightly more emphasis on messianic fulfillment, as the kind of healings Jesus does echo those of the messianic age described in Isaiah 35:5-6. Also, the messianic banquet is to be set on a mountaintop (Isa 25:6-10).

16:1-12 The leaven of the Pharisees and Sadducees

That the feedings of the multitudes were meant to be teaching moments for Jesus' disciples is clear from the dialogue in verses 5-12. This conversation is preceded by a confrontation between Jesus and the religious leaders. By the time Matthew is writing, the Sadducees are no longer an entity. After the destruction of the temple in A.D. 70, their

them in reply, "[In the evening you say, 'Tomorrow will be fair, for the sky is red'; ³and, in the morning, 'Today will be stormy, for the sky is red and threatening.' You know how to judge the appearance of the sky, but you cannot judge the signs of the times.] ⁴An evil and unfaithful generation seeks a sign, but no sign will be given it except the sign of Jonah." Then he left them and went away.

The Leaven of the Pharisees and Sadducees. ⁵In coming to the other side of the sea, the disciples had forgotten to bring bread. ⁶Jesus said to them, "Look out, and beware of the leaven of the Pharisees and Sadducees." ⁷They concluded among themselves, saying, "It is because we have brought no bread."

⁸When Jesus became aware of this he said, "You of little faith, why do you conclude among yourselves that it is because you have no bread? ⁹Do you not yet understand, and do you not remember the five loaves for the five thousand, and how many wicker baskets you took up? ¹⁰Or the seven loaves for the four thousand, and how many baskets you took up? ¹¹How do you not comprehend that I was not speaking to you about bread? Beware of the leaven of the Pharisees and Sadducees." ¹²Then they understood that he was not telling them to beware of the leaven of bread, but of the teaching of the Pharisees and Sadducees.

Peter's Confession about Jesus. ¹³When Jesus went into the region of Caesarea Philippi he asked his disciples,

---

priestly ministry and power base disappeared. Matthew's linking of Pharisees and Sadducees (as at 3:7-10) is a sweeping expression to include all rival religious leaders. Jesus' denunciation of them reflects the conflicts in Matthew's day between the followers of Jesus and those still adhering to synagogue affiliation. The rival religious leaders question Jesus not with sincerity but with the intent to test *(peirazō)* him, as the devil did (4:1, 3). Even though they have signs, they are predisposed not to respond with faith. See 12:38-47 on the sign of Jonah as a reference to Jesus' death and resurrection.

The disciples, in contrast, struggle to move from "little faith" (v. 8; similarly 6:30; 8:26; 14:31) to understanding and belief. Jesus' query about their not remembering (vv. 5, 9) is not so much pointing out a lapse in memory as it is an accusation of disobedience. Unfaithfulness to the covenant is repeatedly spoken of in the Old Testament as forgetfulness of God or of the commandments (e.g., Deut 4:9; 8:11; 9:7; Isa 17:10; Jer 18:15). The symbol of leaven for corruption occurs often in the Scriptures (see 13:33). In contrast to Mark's version of this episode (8:1-10), Matthew's disciples do finally grasp what it is that Jesus, the authoritative teacher, is telling them (v. 12).

Church of the Transfiguration atop Mount Tabor, completed in 1924

"Who do people say that the Son of Man is?" [14]They replied, "Some say John the Baptist, others Elijah, still others Jeremiah or one of the prophets." [15]He said to them, "But who do you say that I am?" [16]Simon Peter said in reply, "You are the Messiah, the Son of the living God." [17]Jesus said to him in reply, "Blessed are you, Simon son of Jonah. For flesh and blood has not revealed this to you, but my heavenly Father. [18]And so I say to you, you are Peter, and upon this rock I will build my church, and the gates of the netherworld shall not prevail against it. [19]I will give you the keys to the kingdom of heaven. Whatever you bind on earth shall be bound in heaven; and whatever you loose on earth shall be loosed in heaven." [20]Then he strictly ordered his disciples to tell no one that he was the Messiah.

The First Prediction of the Passion. [21]From that time on, Jesus began to show his disciples that he must go to Jerusalem and suffer greatly from the elders, the chief priests, and the scribes,

---

JESUS AND HIS DISCIPLES ON THE WAY TO JERUSALEM

Matt 16:13–20:34

16:13-28 Following the Messiah to the cross

This episode constitutes a major turning point in the Gospel. It begins in the northernmost region of Israel, Caesarea Philippi, a city given to Herod the Great by Augustus and rebuilt by Herod's son Philip, who renamed the city after himself and the emperor. The scene moves from the question of Jesus to his disciples about his identity (vv. 13-20), to the first prediction of the passion (vv. 21-23; reiterated at 17:22-23; 20:17-19), to Jesus' instructions to his disciples about taking up the cross (vv. 24-28). The expression "From that time on" (v. 21) signals a major shift in the story. This same phrase, which introduces Jesus' public ministry in Galilee (4:17), now points attention to Jesus' ministry and death in Jerusalem.

On Jesus' identity as "Son of Man" (v. 13) see the comments on 8:20; for his relationship with John the Baptist and Elijah, see 3:1-17; 4:1-11; 9:18-26; 11:1-19; 14:1-12; 17:9-13. Matthew is unique in drawing parallels between Jesus and Jeremiah through his explicit quotations of the prophet (2:17; 27:9) and his allusions to him (7:15-23; 11:28-30; 23:37-39). The declaration of Jesus' messiahship (v. 16) is not a new revelation in Matthew (see 1:1, 17, 18; 11:2). But the nature of Jesus' messiahship as entailing his suffering and death (v. 21) is articulated here for the first time.

As frequently in Matthew, Peter takes a prominent role as spokesperson for the disciples (see also 14:28; 15:15; 17:4, 24-27; 18:21; 19:27; 26:33). The blessing of Peter in verses 17-19 is unique to Matthew. It plays on the

and be killed and on the third day be raised. ²²Then Peter took him aside and began to rebuke him, "God forbid, Lord! No such thing shall ever happen to you." ²³He turned and said to Peter, "Get behind me, Satan! You are an obstacle to me. You are thinking not as God does, but as human beings do."

The Conditions of Discipleship. ²⁴Then Jesus said to his disciples, "Whoever wishes to come after me must deny himself, take up his cross, and follow me. ²⁵For whoever wishes to save his life will lose it, but whoever loses his life for my sake will find it. ²⁶What profit would there be for one to gain the whole world and forfeit his life? Or what can one give in exchange for his life? ²⁷For the Son of Man will come with his angels in his Father's glory, and then he will repay everyone according to his conduct. ²⁸Amen, I say to you, there are some standing here who will not taste death until they see the Son of Man coming in his kingdom."

---

meaning of his name, *Petros* ("rock") in Greek, *Cephas* in Aramaic (1 Cor 15:5), and counters the worship for which Caesarea Philippi was known. It had a sanctuary for the god Pan, with a large rock-faced cliff with carved niches that held statues. Jesus' blessing of Peter exalts the emerging rock-like faith, not only of Peter but of the whole community of disciples. This is the unshakable foundation (see 7:24-27) for those who cling to the "stone that the builders rejected" (21:42; Ps 118:22). Jesus assures the community that God will stand behind their decisions about membership, regulations, and forgiveness (see 18:18, where all the members are given the power to "bind" and to "loose").

Peter's reaction to Jesus' prediction of the passion highlights the fact that the formation of the disciples is not yet complete. The "rock" falters when confronted with the stumbling block (*skandalon*, 18:6, 7) of the passion. Jesus then builds on the instructions begun at 10:38-39 in the mission discourse. To be his disciple entails willingness to lose even life itself. To take up one's cross does not refer to enduring whatever suffering comes in life; rather, it refers specifically to the willingness to suffer the consequences for proclaiming and living the Gospel. So it is not a saying that encourages persons who are victimized or suffering to simply bear it as their way of identifying with Jesus.

As we have seen in the Gospel, Jesus always healed and alleviated the suffering of all such persons. Likewise the saying about denial of self is not simply self-denial in the sense of choosing to giving up certain pleasures; rather, it concerns the disciples' choice to lose themselves entirely in Christ—to take on his way of life and mission and his very identity as one's own. Paradoxically, this is the way that truly leads to life. A

17 The Transfiguration of Jesus.

¹After six days Jesus took Peter, James, and John his brother, and led them up a high mountain by themselves. ²And he was transfigured before them; his face shone like the sun and his clothes became white as light. ³And behold, Moses and Elijah appeared to them, conversing with him. ⁴Then Peter said to Jesus in reply, "Lord, it is good that we are here. If you wish, I will make three tents here, one for you, one for Moses, and one for Elijah." ⁵While he was still speaking, behold, a bright cloud cast a shadow over them, then from the cloud came a voice that said, "This is my beloved Son, with whom I am well pleased; listen to him." ⁶When the disciples heard this, they fell prostrate and were very much afraid. ⁷But Jesus came and touched them, saying, "Rise, and do not be afraid." ⁸And when the disciples raised their eyes, they saw no one else but Jesus alone.

The Coming of Elijah. ⁹As they were coming down from the mountain, Jesus charged them, "Do not tell the vision to anyone until the Son of Man has been raised from the dead." ¹⁰Then the disciples asked him, "Why do the scribes say that Elijah must come first?" ¹¹He said in reply, "Elijah will indeed come and restore all things; ¹²but I tell you that Elijah has already come, and they did not recognize him but did to him whatever they pleased. So also will the Son of

---

reminder about judgment and the imminent coming of the Son of Humanity (vv. 27-28) underscores that the choice to follow Jesus or not carries eternal consequences.

17:1-13 The transfiguration of Jesus and the coming of Elijah

The question of Jesus' identity and what that means continues to loom large in this episode. On the heels of Jesus' teaching that he must suffer and die and then be raised up (16:21), the reader is given utter assurance that Jesus' execution does not mean that he is accursed (Deut 21:23) or in any way rejected by God. The brilliance of his face and clothing (v. 2) indicates his righteousness (see 13:43). The voice from heaven (v. 5) reaffirms the message heard at Jesus' baptism (3:17): he is God's beloved one. The instruction "listen to him" (v. 5) echoes Deuteronomy 18:15 and insists that Jesus is the correct interpreter of the Law and the Prophets, signified by the figures of Moses and Elijah (v. 3).

Matthew further highlights the portrait of Jesus as the new Moses with the details of the high mountain (v. 1; see also 5:1; 15:29; 28:16), Jesus' shining face (v. 2, like that of Moses after his encounter with God on Mount Sinai, Exod 34:29), and the overshadowing cloud (v. 5, like that which signaled God's presence with Israel in their sojourn to freedom, Exod 16:10; 19:9, etc.). Matthew specifically labels this experience a vision (v. 9), and

Man suffer at their hands." ¹³Then the disciples understood that he was speaking to them of John the Baptist.

The Healing of a Boy with a Demon. ¹⁴When they came to the crowd a man approached, knelt down before him, ¹⁵and said, "Lord, have pity on my son, for he is a lunatic and suffers severely; often he falls into fire, and often into water. ¹⁶I brought him to your disciples, but they could not cure him." ¹⁷Jesus said in reply, "O faithless and perverse generation, how long will I be with you? How long will I endure you? Bring him here to me." ¹⁸Jesus rebuked him and the demon came out of him, and from that hour the boy was cured. ¹⁹Then the disciples approached Jesus in private and said, "Why could we not drive it out?" ²⁰He said to them, "Because of your little faith. Amen, I say to you, if you have faith the size of a mustard seed, you will say to this mountain, 'Move from here to there,' and it will move. Nothing will be impossible for you."[²¹]

The Second Prediction of the Passion. ²²As they were gathering in Galilee, Jesus said to them, "The Son of Man is to be handed over to men, ²³and ▶

---

the disciples react in much the same way as Daniel did to his apocalyptic visions (Dan 8:17-18; 10:7-9).

The discussion about Elijah (vv. 9-13) reflects a debate about the correct interpretation of Malachi 4:5 (3:23 Hebrew), which speaks about the coming of Elijah before the Day of the Lord. For Christians this has taken place in the person of John the Baptist (see also 3:1-17; 9:18-26; 11:1-19; 14:1-12).

17:14-20 The power of little faith

The tragic situation of a child who suffers from what is probably epilepsy (the Greek word *selēniazomai* literally means "moonstruck") becomes an occasion for further training for the disciples. The father's plaintive "Lord, have pity" echoes the pleas of other sufferers in the Gospel (8:2, 5-6, 25; 14:30; 15:22, 25; 20:30-31). While the disciples have been given the authority to cure every disease and illness (10:1), Matthew has not yet reported that they were ever able to do so (cf. Mark 6:13, 30). Jesus' harsh words for the disciples echo those of Moses as he voiced his exasperation with Israel (Deut 32:5). Jesus redirects the disciples away from focusing on what they lack, toward claiming and exercising the power they do have with their little faith (see also 6:30; 8:26; 14:31; 16:8; 21:21-22). See 13:31-32 for the parable of the mustard seed.

17:22-23 Second prediction of the Passion

The reaction of the disciples to this second prediction of Jesus' death and resurrection is not denial, as in 16:21-23, but overwhelming grief.

they will kill him, and he will be raised on the third day." And they were overwhelmed with grief.

Payment of the Temple Tax. ²⁴When they came to Capernaum, the collectors of the temple tax approached Peter and said, "Doesn't your teacher pay the temple tax?" ²⁵"Yes," he said. When he came into the house, before he had time to speak, Jesus asked him, "What is your opinion, Simon? From whom do the kings of the earth take tolls or census tax? From their subjects or from foreigners?" ²⁶When he said, "From foreigners," Jesus said to him, "Then the subjects are exempt. ²⁷But that we may not offend them, go to the sea, drop in a hook, and take the first fish that comes up. Open its mouth and you will find a coin worth twice the temple tax. Give that to them for me and for you."

18 The Greatest in the Kingdom. ¹At that time the disciples approached Jesus and said, "Who is the greatest in the kingdom of heaven?" ²He called a child over, placed it in their midst, ³and said, "Amen, I say to you, unless you turn and become like children, you will not enter the kingdom of heaven. ⁴Whoever humbles himself like this child is the greatest in the kingdom of heaven. ⁵And whoever receives one child such as this in my name receives me.

Temptations to Sin. ⁶"Whoever causes one of these little ones who believe in me to sin, it would be better for him to have a great millstone hung around his neck and to be drowned in

---

Their progress in comprehension and acceptance advances as they move with Jesus toward Jerusalem (contrast Mark 9:2).

17:24-27 The temple tax

This story is peculiar to Matthew's Gospel. The issue is the payment of a yearly tax of a half-shekel that was obligatory for all Jewish males over twenty years old (Exod 30:11-16). This served for the upkeep of the temple, as well as a sign of solidarity among Jews both within Israel and in the Diaspora. Controversy over this payment may have stemmed from disapproval over the manner in which the money was used by the Sadducees or the shaming of those who were too poor to contribute. Jesus' exchange with Peter makes it clear that as children of God, whose house the temple is, they are exempt from taxes for the temple. Nonetheless, for the sake of not causing scandal, Jesus pays the money. The fantastic detail of finding a coin in the mouth of a fish gives the story the air of a folktale.

18:1-14 Greatness in God's realm

The fourth great block of teaching concerns life in community. The first section (18:1-14) focuses on the need for humility and for the care of the

the depths of the sea. ⁷Woe to the world because of things that cause sin! Such things must come, but woe to the one through whom they come! ⁸If your hand or foot causes you to sin, cut it off and throw it away. It is better for you to enter into life maimed or crippled than with two hands or two feet to be thrown into eternal fire. ⁹And if your eye causes you to sin, tear it out and throw it away. It is better for you to enter into life with one eye than with two eyes to be thrown into fiery Gehenna.

The Parable of the Lost Sheep. ¹⁰"See that you do not despise one of these little ones, for I say to you that their angels in heaven always look upon the face of my heavenly Father. [¹¹] ¹²What is your opinion? If a man has a hundred sheep and one of them goes astray, will he not leave the ninety-nine in the hills and go in search of the stray? ¹³And if he finds it, amen, I say to you, he rejoices

most vulnerable. The second (18:15-20) outlines a procedure for reconciling aggrieved members of the community, followed by a parable (18:21-35) about unlimited forgiveness. While these teachings are addressed to "the disciples" (v. 1), the nature of the instruction is to those with leadership responsibility, not to the "little ones."

In the first part (vv. 1-5) Jesus teaches leaders to cultivate humility by consciously identifying themselves with the concerns of the least important in the community. Children are certainly valued in families, but they are the most vulnerable and the least able to contribute to the sustenance of the group, at least until they are older. A second way to exercise humility is by showing hospitality toward those who are "nobodies" (v. 5). Lavishing care on them with the same attentiveness and openness that one would show to an important guest is the way of true leadership. Finally, leaders must be wary of putting any stumbling block (*skandalon*, vv. 6-9) in the way of a "little one." The consequences for doing so are dire. Matthew does not spell out precisely who the "little ones" are. They may be new converts or those whose faith is not yet strong. At 10:42 they are Christian missionaries. One's treatment of "the least" is the basis for reward or punishment at the last judgment (25:40, 45).

A further lesson in prizing each of the "little ones" is presented in the parable of the shepherd who goes to extraordinary lengths to recover a lost sheep (vv. 10-14). Christian leaders are to emulate God's care for Israel (Ps 23; Isa 40:11) and Jesus' compassion for people who are "like sheep without a shepherd" (9:36). They are not to be like the shepherds that Ezekiel (34:12) denounces for placing their own welfare above that of the "flock." They are to seek out the "lost sheep of the house of Israel" (10:6).

more over it than over the ninety-nine that did not stray. ¹⁴In just the same way, it is not the will of your heavenly Father that one of these little ones be lost.

A Brother Who Sins. ¹⁵"If your brother sins [against you], go and tell him his fault between you and him alone. If he listens to you, you have won over your brother. ¹⁶If he does not listen, take one or two others along with you, so that 'every fact may be established on the testimony of two or three witnesses.' ¹⁷If he refuses to listen to them, tell the church. If he refuses to listen even to the church, then treat him as you would a Gentile or a tax collector. ¹⁸Amen, I say to you, whatever you bind on earth shall be bound in heaven, and whatever you loose on earth shall be loosed in heaven. ¹⁹Again, [amen,] I say to you, if two of you agree on earth about anything for which they are to pray, it shall be granted to them by my heavenly Father. ²⁰For where two or three are gathered together in my name, there am I in the midst of them."

The Parable of the Unforgiving Servant. ²¹Then Peter approaching

The emphasis in Matthew's version of the parable is not on the repentance of the sheep (cf. Luke 15:7), but rather on the urgent task of the shepherd who follows God's will and experiences great joy in finding the lost (vv. 13-14).

18:15-20 A process for reconciliation

This section presents steps to be taken in the community when one member sins against another. The first step is direct confrontation, begun by the one who is offended (v. 15) and approaches the other with a willingness to forgive. The best case scenario is that this first confrontation brings about the needed repentance, and then reconciliation results. If it fails, however, the next step is to involve one or two others from the community (v. 16). The aim is to establish the truth, relying on impartial witnesses or facilitators. If this does not work, then the matter is brought before the whole community (*ekklēsia*, "church," used only here and in 16:18 in the Gospels). If that fails, then the person is to be treated like "a Gentile or a tax collector" (v. 17). It is not clear whether this means to exclude the person or to emulate Jesus' practice of befriending such people (see 8:5-13; 9:9-13; 11:19; 15:21-28).

Here Jesus may be advocating that Christians be willing to sit and break bread together, even while they are working toward resolving their differences. Note that Matthew does not indicate the nature of the offense. Such a strategy would not work for every kind of sin. Note that the whole community has a role in binding and loosing offenses (18:18), and the whole body is involved in praying for reconciliation.

asked him, "Lord, if my brother sins against me, how often must I forgive him? As many as seven times?" ²²Jesus answered, "I say to you, not seven times but seventy-seven times. ²³That is why the kingdom of heaven may be likened to a king who decided to settle accounts with his servants. ²⁴When he began the accounting, a debtor was brought before him who owed him a huge amount. ²⁵Since he had no way of paying it back, his master ordered him to be sold, along with his wife, his children, and all his property, in payment of the debt. ²⁶At that, the servant fell down, did him homage, and said, 'Be patient with me, and I will pay you back in full.' ²⁷Moved with compassion the master of that servant let him go and forgave him the loan. ²⁸When that servant had left, he found one of his fellow servants who owed him a much smaller amount. He seized him and started to choke him, demanding, 'Pay back what you owe.' ²⁹Falling to his knees, his fellow servant begged him, 'Be patient with me, and I will pay you back.' ³⁰But he refused. Instead, he had him put in prison until he paid back the debt. ³¹Now when his fellow servants saw what had happened, they were deeply disturbed, and went to their master and reported the whole affair. ³²His master summoned him and said to him, 'You wicked servant! I forgave you your entire debt because you begged me to. ³³Should you not have had pity on your fellow servant, as I had pity on you?' ³⁴Then in anger his master handed him over to the torturers until he should pay back the whole debt. ³⁵So will my heavenly Father do

18:21-35 Forgiveness aborted

The process sketched above is lengthy and arduous. Peter asks Jesus how often you have to do all this—as many as seven times? In biblical terms, seven is a perfect number, signifying here an endless number of times. Jesus' exhortation to forgive seventy-seven times (v. 22) contrasts with the threat of Lamech, who vowed vengeance "seventy-sevenfold" (Gen 4:24).

The parable plays out in three acts. In the first (vv. 23-27) a king decides to call in his "loan" *(daneion)*, that is, the money due him from a slave who is a high-level bureaucrat (indicated by the amounts of money with which he deals, v. 24). This slave is evidently responsible for exacting tribute from other subjects. He builds networks and works the system to his and the king's advantage. The king, in a pure display of power, wants to collect ten thousand talents, approximately six to ten thousand days' wages. His purpose is to remind the servant of his subservience. The slave's response is exactly what the king wanted (v. 26). He does homage to the king and acknowledges his dependence and loyalty. The king is satisfied and returns him to his position. Word will spread both of the king's power and his generosity.

to you, unless each of you forgives his brother from his heart."

VI. Ministry in Judea and Jerusalem

◄ 19 **Marriage and Divorce.** ¹When Jesus finished these words, he left Galilee and went to the district of Judea across the Jordan. ²Great crowds followed him, and he cured them there. ³Some Pharisees approached him, and ▷ tested him, saying, "Is it lawful for a man to divorce his wife for any cause whatever?" ⁴He said in reply, "Have ▷ you not read that from the beginning the Creator 'made them male and female' ⁵and said, 'For this reason a man

---

In the second act (vv. 28-30) the forgiven bureaucrat replicates the king's actions with his subordinates. This one owes him one hundred times less than the amount he owed the king. The point is not the difference in amount but that both are unable to pay. Although the second underling responds in exactly the same way his master did to the king, the latter carries through his threats with a vengeance instead of forgiving the debt.

In the final part (vv. 31-34) the fellow servants report everything to the king, who becomes enraged. If his servant has understood the meaning of his previous actions, then he should have replicated them. If the slave wants loyalty, adulation, and recognition of his power, the king has shown him how to exact it. Instead, he has shamed the king by not imitating him. He has said by his actions that the king's method of exerting power is not effective. If the slave thinks that physical abuse, debasing another, and brutal imprisonment are the ways to gain power, then the king will show him just that. The conclusion (v. 35) was likely added by the evangelist.

As with all metaphors, the king is both like and unlike God. Unlike the monarch in the parable, God does not work for his own self-aggrandizement, but for the well-being of all creation. But like the king, God, through Jesus, has graciously forgiven all debt of sin (for which Jesus teaches the disciples to pray in 6:12). The only response to such mercy is to let it transform one's heart so as to be able to act with the same kind of graciousness toward others. This kind of power is through vulnerability and a willingness to forgo vengeance to work toward reconciliation. Those who do not learn to imitate godly ways in their dealings with one another will be treated by God in the way they have treated others.

19:1-15 Teaching on divorce and blessing of children

In his journey toward Jerusalem, Jesus takes the route along the eastern side of the Jordan River, as did most Jews, to avoid going through Samaria (v. 1). As at 16:1, rival religious leaders put a question to Jesus to

shall leave his father and mother and be joined to his wife, and the two shall ◄ become one flesh'? ⁶So they are no longer two, but one flesh. Therefore, what God has joined together, no ◄ human being must separate." ⁷They said to him, "Then why did Moses command that the man give the woman a bill of divorce and dismiss ◄ [her]?" ⁸He said to them, "Because of the hardness of your hearts Moses allowed you to divorce your wives, but from the beginning it was not so. ⁹I say to you, whoever divorces his wife (unless the marriage is unlawful) and mar- ◄ ries another commits adultery." ¹⁰[His] disciples said to him, "If that is the case of a man with his wife, it is better not to marry." ¹¹He answered, "Not all can ac- ► cept [this] word, but only those to whom that is granted. ¹²Some are inca- ► pable of marriage because they were born so; some, because they were made so by others; some, because they have renounced marriage for the sake of the kingdom of heaven. Whoever can accept this ought to accept it."

Blessing of the Children. ¹³Then children were brought to him that he might lay his hands on them and pray. The disciples rebuked them, ¹⁴but Jesus said, "Let the children come to me, and do not prevent them; for the kingdom of heaven belongs to such as these." ¹⁵After he placed his hands on them, he went away.

---

test him (*peirazō*, as also 4:1, 3). Jesus' teaching on not divorcing was already introduced in the Sermon on the Mount (5:31-32). Now the question centers on whether there are any exceptions (v. 3). The exchange is cast as a rabbinical debate, such as the one between the first-century rabbis Shammai and Hillel. The latter held that a man could divorce his wife even for spoiling a dish for him, whereas the former argued that only sexual misconduct was grounds for divorce.

In his reply Jesus first cites Genesis 1:27 and then Genesis 2:24, arguing that God's intention from creation is for man and woman to remain united. Jesus' opponents, also citing Scripture, come back with a text from Deuteronomy 24:1-4, where Moses permits a man to divorce his wife by handing her a written bill of divorce. Jesus distinguishes between God's positive command in Genesis, which reveals God's intent, and Moses' concession to Israel because of their inability to achieve the ideal. As at 5:32, Jesus characterizes divorce as adultery, unless the basis for separating is *porneia* (v. 9). The meaning of this word is not certain. It may refer to sexual misconduct, such as adultery or marriage to close kin, which was forbidden in Jewish law (Lev 18:6-18; see also Acts 15:20, 29). If it is the latter, then the question concerns some Gentile converts who wished to become Christian but who were in such forbidden marriages. Would they first have to divorce to enter the community?

The Rich Young Man. [16]Now someone approached him and said, "Teacher, what good must I do to gain eternal life?" [17]He answered him, "Why do you ask me about the good? There is only One who is good. If you wish to enter into life, keep the commandments." [18]He asked him, "Which ones?" And Jesus replied, " 'You shall not kill; you shall not commit adultery; you shall not steal; you shall not bear false witness; [19]honor your father and your mother'; and 'you shall love your neighbor as yourself.' " [20]The young man said to him, "All of these I have observed. What do I still lack?" [21]Jesus said to him, "If you wish to be perfect, go, sell what you have and give to [the] poor, and you will have treasure in heaven. Then come, follow me." [22]When the young man heard this statement, he went away sad, for he had

---

The reaction of Jesus' disciples reveals the radical nature of his teaching. "It is better not to marry" (v. 10) is akin to the hyperbole in 18:8-9, which states that it is better to cut off a hand or foot or eye rather than cause a little one to sin. Jesus acknowledges that not all can accept this teaching. It has long been debated whether the saying in verse 12 refers to those who choose to remain celibate or to those who do not remarry after the death or divorce of a spouse. In Jewish tradition marriage was the norm, although some groups, such as the Therapeutae and the Qumranites, evidently practiced celibacy.

The reason why a Christian might make such a choice is for the sake of the mission. Many widows in the early church chose to live together and to devote themselves to ministry rather than remarry (see Acts 9:39, which may refer to such a situation, and 1 Timothy 5:3-16 for regulations regarding them). For women in Jesus' day, his stricter teaching on divorce may often have served a compassionate end, safeguarding women from being cast aside for no good reason and from being placed in a vulnerable position socially and economically. By the same token, painful decisions about divorce in a contemporary context must take into consideration Jesus' prime concern for the well-being of each person as a valued son or daughter of God in the community of believers.

In verses 13-15 the lens widens to the most vulnerable members in the family unit. When linked to the previous scene, Jesus' blessing and prayer for the little ones recognize that they may be the ones who suffer most when the parents are contemplating divorce. A reason why the disciples wanted to prevent the children from coming to Jesus is not given. In a pronouncement reminiscent of 18:3, Jesus speaks about their importance in God's realm.

many possessions. [23]Then Jesus said to his disciples, "Amen, I say to you, it will be hard for one who is rich to enter the kingdom of heaven. [24]Again I say to you, it is easier for a camel to pass through the eye of a needle than for one who is rich to enter the kingdom of God." [25]When the disciples heard this, they were greatly astonished and said, "Who then can be saved?" [26]Jesus looked at them and said, "For human beings this is impossible, but for God all things are possible." [27]Then Peter said to him in reply, "We have given up everything and followed you. What will there be for us?" [28]Jesus said to them, "Amen, I say to you that you who have followed me, in the new age, when the Son of Man is seated on his throne of glory, will yourselves sit on twelve thrones, judging the twelve tribes of Israel. [29]And everyone who has given up houses or brothers or sisters or father or mother or children or lands for the sake of my name will receive a hundred times more, and will

19:16-30 Discipleship and possessions

The exchange between Jesus and the rich young man and the ensuing discussion with the disciples speak soberly about the obstacle that possessions can pose for discipleship. In Matthew's account (cf. Mark 10:17-31; Luke 18:18-30), the rich man asks Jesus about doing good, one of the evangelist's favorite themes (5:16; 7:17-19; 12:12, 33-35; 13:23, 24; 26:10). Keeping the commandments is a first step in doing good. The young man's question, "Which ones?" rings false, since all the commandments must be kept equally. Jesus' invitation to him to go beyond simply keeping the commandments and to "be perfect" (*teleios*, as also at 5:48) concerns becoming "whole" or "complete." As at 5:48, this is not an invitation for a select few, nor is it presenting a contrast between Judaism and Christianity. In the Old Testament, although riches are regarded as a sign of God's blessing (Deut 28:1-14), there are also the same dire warnings about the corrosiveness of riches (Ezek 7:19; Amos 6:4-8; Prov 15:16).

In Matthew's perspective, being a disciple of Jesus entails faithfulness to the Jewish Law as interpreted by Jesus, which demands radical attachment to him. It is as difficult for a rich person to do this as it is for a camel to squeeze through the eye of a needle (v. 24). The popular interpretation that there was a gate so named in Jerusalem has no basis. Jesus' response to the disciples' astonishment (similarly, 19:10) is to refocus their attention on God's initiative and power with them, enabling them to do what is good—the question with which the rich man began (v. 16). See also the beatitude of the poor in 6:3 and the admonitions that the heart lies where the treasure is (6:21) and that one cannot serve both God and mammon (6:24). The treasure to seek above all is the realm of God (13:44). The theme of

inherit eternal life. ³⁰But many who are first will be last, and the last will be first.

20 **The Workers in the Vineyard.** ¹"The kingdom of heaven is like a landowner who went out at dawn to hire laborers for his vineyard. ²After agreeing with them for the usual daily wage, he sent them into his vineyard. ³Going out about nine o'clock, he saw others standing idle in the marketplace, ⁴and he said to them, 'You too go into my vineyard, and I will give you what is just.' ⁵So they went off. [And] he went out again around noon, and around three o'clock, and did likewise. ⁶Going out about five o'clock, he found others standing around, and said to them, 'Why do you stand here idle all day?' ⁷They answered, 'Because no one has hired us.' He said to them, 'You too go into my vineyard.' ⁸When it was evening the owner of the vineyard said to his foreman, 'Summon the laborers and give them their pay, beginning with the last and ending with the first.' ⁹When those who had started about five o'clock came, each received the usual daily wage. ¹⁰So when the first came, they thought that they would re-

reward for disciples runs throughout the Gospel (5:12, 46-47; 6:1-6, 16, 18; 10:39-42; 25:21, 23, 34). Here the focus is eschatological. Disciples share in the glory and the final judgment by the Human One, as their self-emptying for God's realm has prepared them to receive the eternal inheritance God wills for all.

20:1-16 Justice in the vineyard

This parable and the previous episode conclude with the same saying about reversal (19:30; 20:16). This is a floating proverb that is tagged on to various New Testament passages in diverse contexts (see also Mark 10:31; Luke 13:30). It does not supply the meaning for the parable. In the story the first hired are paid last because the point of the story depends on their seeing what the last hired receive. The complaint of the workers in verse 12 voices what is so puzzling about this parable. Does not justice demand that those who worked more earn more? The vineyard owner has promised that he will pay what is just (*dikaios*, v. 4) and insists that he is doing no injustice (*ouk adikō se*, v. 13). He then asks, "Am I not free to do as I wish with my own money? Are you envious because I am generous?" (v. 15).

Two important points are made in the landowner's reply. If he is a figure for God, his actions show that God's generosity, which is not merited, is freely lavished on those most in need. God's generosity does no injustice, but neither can it be calculated or earned. The story *is* about people getting what they deserve: all have the right to eat for the day. From the position of the day laborers, who are on the lowest economic rung and

ceive more, but each of them also got the usual wage. [11]And on receiving it they grumbled against the landowner, [12]saying, 'These last ones worked only one hour, and you have made them equal to us, who bore the day's burden and the heat.' [13]He said to one of them in reply, 'My friend, I am not cheating you. Did you not agree with me for the usual daily wage? [14]Take what is yours and go. What if I wish to give this last one the same as you? [15][Or] am I not free to do as I wish with my own money? Are you envious because I am generous?' [16]Thus, the last will be first, and the first will be last."

The Third Prediction of the Passion. [17]As Jesus was going up to Jerusalem, he took the twelve [disciples] aside by themselves, and said to them on the way, [18]"Behold, we are going up to Jerusalem, and the Son of Man will be handed over to the chief priests and the scribes, and they will condemn him to death, [19]and hand him over to the Gentiles to be mocked and scourged ▶

who stand waiting all day (v. 6), wanting to work but not hired, the wage given them enables them to feed their family for one more day. Less than a denarius would be useless. From their perspective, those who were hired at the beginning of the day, though they have worked longer and harder, at least had the satisfaction of knowing all day that come sundown they would be able to feed their families. In God's realm, justice means that all are fed as a sign of God's equal and inclusive love; it does not mean getting what we deserve, either in terms of retribution for wrongdoing or recompense for good deeds.

The second point is that "evil-eye" envy is the most destructive force in a community. The question in verse 15 is, literally, "Or is your eye evil that I am good?" In a first-century worldview of limited good, anyone's gain means another one's loss. While the grumblers focus on their perceived loss, they miss the limitless goodness and generosity of the landowner. Linked with the previous discussion about the danger of riches, this parable challenges those disciples who have enough to meet their daily needs to reject acquisitiveness and attend to the needs of those who are in desperate straits.

20:17-28 To drink the cup

The third prediction of Jesus' passion is more detailed than the others and occurs as Jesus and his disciples near Jerusalem. In the first prediction (16:21-23) Jesus told his disciples that he would be killed at the hands of the elders, chief priests, and scribes. In fact, the Jewish leaders did not have the authority to carry out capital punishment (see John 18:31). Jesus will actually be handed over to the Gentiles (v. 19), who will put him to

and crucified, and he will be raised on the third day."

The Request of James and John. ²⁰Then the mother of the sons of Zebedee approached him with her sons and did him homage, wishing to ask him for something. ²¹He said to her, "What do you wish?" She answered him, "Command that these two sons of mine sit, one at your right and the other at your left, in your kingdom." ²²Jesus said in reply, "You do not know what you are asking. Can you drink the cup that I am going to drink?" They said to him, "We can." ²³He replied, "My cup you will indeed drink, but to sit at my right and at my left [, this] is not mine to give but is for those for whom it has been prepared by my Father." ²⁴When the ten heard this, they became indignant at the two brothers. ²⁵But Jesus summoned them and said, "You know that the rulers of the Gentiles lord it over them, and the great ones make their authority over them felt. ²⁶But it shall not be so among you. Rather, whoever wishes to be great among you shall be your servant; ²⁷whoever wishes

death (cf. the second prediction, where Jesus spoke in general terms of being betrayed into human hands, 17:22-23).

It is jarring to have the disciples bickering over the places of honor in the kingdom after this sober prediction. Matthew redacts the story (cf. Mark 10:35-45), so that the mother of James and John makes the request, thus softening the critique of the disciples and making their mother the ambitious one. It is ambiguous whether the other ten are indignant at the audacity of the request or whether they are upset that these two beat them to it (v. 24).

The metaphor "cup" is used often in the Scriptures to speak of the suffering of Israel (Isa 51:17; Jer 25:15; 49:12; 51:7; Lam 4:21; *Mart. Isa.* 5:13). In 26:39 Jesus implores God to let "this cup" pass him by. Jesus then instructs the disciples on the manner of leadership they are to exercise. They are not to "lord it over" any others; rather, like Jesus himself, they are to serve the rest of the community. Jesus' service is service to the death, a giving of his life as ransom for all. The word *polys*, "many," does not exclude anyone. It reflects a Semitic expression where "many" is the opposite of "one," thus the equivalent of "all." The notion of Jesus giving his life as ransom draws on the image of a slave who buys back his freedom for a price. These last verses of the Gospel are aimed at leaders who have some degree of power, privilege, status, and choice. Their choice to take the lowly position of service is liberating when accompanied by empowerment of those who are otherwise powerless. These sayings must not be used to reinforce the servitude of those who are enslaved in whatever way.

An olive grove on the Mount of Olives

to be first among you shall be your slave. [28]Just so, the Son of Man did not come to be served but to serve and to give his life as a ransom for many."

The Healing of Two Blind Men. [29]As they left Jericho, a great crowd followed him. [30]Two blind men were sitting by the roadside, and when they heard that Jesus was passing by, they cried out, "[Lord,] Son of David, have pity on us!" [31]The crowd warned them to be silent, but they called out all the more, "Lord, Son of David, have pity on us!" [32]Jesus stopped and called them and said, "What do you want me to do for you?" [33]They answered him, "Lord, let our eyes be opened." [34]Moved with pity, Jesus touched their eyes. Immediately they received their sight, and followed him.

21 **The Entry into Jerusalem.** [1]When they drew near Jerusalem and came to Bethphage on the Mount of Olives, Jesus sent two disciples, [2]saying to them, "Go into the village opposite you, and immediately you will find an ass tethered, and a colt with her. Untie them and bring them here to me. [3]And if anyone should say anything to you, reply, 'The master has need of them.' Then he will send them at once." [4]This happened so that what had been spoken through the prophet might be fulfilled:

[5]"Say to daughter Zion,
'Behold, your king comes to you,
meek and riding on an ass,
and on a colt, the foal of a
beast of burden.'"
[6]The disciples went and did as Jesus had ordered them. [7]They brought the

---

20:29-34 A final healing

This is the last healing story in the Gospel. It mirrors the one in 9:27-31, where two blind men also cried out to Jesus, "Son of David, have pity on us!" (see also 12:23; 15:22). After having instructed his disciples on servant leadership (20:25-28), Jesus demonstrates for them the kind of descendant of King David he is. As in 9:27-31, Jesus engages the two men in conversation; he does not merely touch them and keep going. Jesus treats them not simply as objects of compassion but with dignity, as people who are able to articulate their need (v. 32). These two who see and follow (v. 34) model the response needed of disciples as Jesus now prepares to enter Jerusalem as Son of David (21:9, 15) to begin the ordeal that will culminate in his reign with God.

JERUSALEM; JESUS' FINAL DAYS OF TEACHING IN THE TEMPLE

Matt 21:1–28:15

21:1-11 Entry into Jerusalem

Jesus' journey to Jerusalem, begun at 16:21, climaxes with his enthusiastic reception by a very large crowd (vv. 1-11), and his action in the

ass and the colt and laid their cloaks over them, and he sat upon them. ⁸The very large crowd spread their cloaks on the road, while others cut branches from the trees and strewed them on the road. ⁹The crowds preceding him and those following kept crying out and saying:

> "Hosanna to the Son of David;
> blessed is he who comes in the
> name of the Lord;
> hosanna in the highest."

¹⁰And when he entered Jerusalem the whole city was shaken and asked, "Who is this?" ¹¹And the crowds replied, "This is Jesus the prophet, from Nazareth in Galilee."

The Cleansing of the Temple. ¹²Jesus entered the temple area and drove out all those engaged in selling and buying there. He overturned the tables of the money changers and the seats of those who were selling doves. ¹³And he said to them, "It is written:

> 'My house shall be a house of
> prayer,'
> but you are making it a den of
> thieves."

¹⁴The blind and the lame approached him in the temple area, and he cured them. ¹⁵When the chief priests and the scribes saw the wondrous things he was doing, and the children crying out in the temple area, "Hosanna to the Son of David," they were indignant ¹⁶and said to him, "Do you hear what they are saying?" Jesus said to them, "Yes; and have you never read the text, 'Out of the mouths of infants and nurslings you have brought forth praise'?" ¹⁷And

temple (vv. 12-17). Both scenes are eschatological in tone and are heavily interlaced with quotations from the prophets, so that the significance in terms of fulfillment of Scriptures is most evident. Jesus enters the city from the east. The Mount of Olives, according to Zechariah 14:4 is the place where the final eschatological struggle will take place. Matthew seems to speak of two animals (v. 2), but he is preserving the parallelism of Zechariah 9:9 (quoted in v. 5), which actually describes only one beast. The prophet tells of the Messiah entering the city "riding on an ass, / on a colt, the foal of an ass." Jesus' action is a parody of that of a conqueror over a vanquished city. The Hebrew word *hôšiʾânā'* means "save, please!" Here it is not so much a plea for help as an acclamation of praise. The shouts of adulation of the crowd (echoing Ps 118:26 in v. 9) contrast with the mounting antagonism of the Jewish leaders. The reaction described in verse 10, "the whole city was shaken *(eseisthē)*," points ahead to the aftermath of the death of Jesus, when "the earth quaked *(eseisthē)*," 27:51).

21:12-17 Confrontation in the temple

In Matthew's account, Jesus' entry into Jerusalem culminates with his action in the temple (cf. Mark 11:15-19, where Jesus waits until the next

leaving them, he went out of the city to Bethany, and there he spent the night.

The Cursing of the Fig Tree. [18]When he was going back to the city in the morning, he was hungry. [19]Seeing a fig tree by the road, he went over to it, but found nothing on it except leaves. And he said to it, "May no fruit ever come from you again." And immediately the fig tree withered. [20]When the disciples saw this, they were amazed and said, "How was it that the fig tree withered immediately?" [21]Jesus said to them in reply, "Amen, I say to you, if you have faith and do not waver, not only will you do what has been done to the fig tree, but even if you say to this mountain, 'Be lifted up and thrown into the

---

day). Scholars still speculate on the nature of the abuse that Jesus was protesting. The interpretation of each evangelist differs slightly. In Matthew's account, Jesus interrupts the commercial activity in the temple area (v. 12). Buying and selling of animals was necessary for temple sacrifice. Doves were the poor woman's offering after childbirth (Lev 12:6-8; Luke 2:24). Greek and Roman coins had to be changed into Tyrian shekels, not because they lacked an offensive image, but because they had the highest silver content.

Matthew interprets Jesus' action (v. 13) by combining quotations from Isaiah 56:7and Jeremiah 7:11. The first speaks of the messianic ideal of the temple being a perfect place of prayer for all peoples (though Matthew omits that last phrase; cf. Mark 11:16). The second was a warning to the people of Judah, who continued trusting in the efficacy of temple worship while their deeds toward one another were rampantly unjust. Jeremiah warned that their corruption was defiling their "hideout," the temple, and predicted its destruction. In verses 12-13 Matthew's Jesus is a fiery prophet bent on rectifying abuse. In verses 14-17, unique to Matthew, Jesus is the compassionate healer of those who are least welcome in the temple (see Lev 21:18, where the blind and the lame are forbidden to offer sacrifices).

Jesus fulfills the messianic promise of Isaiah 35:5-6, where all, including those who are blind and lame, are healed and march exultantly into Jerusalem. Typically, the response to Jesus is divided. The leaders become indignant, while the children (see also 18:1-4; 19:13-15) sing "Hosanna to the Son of David" (see the use of this title in healing stories at 9:27; 12:23; 15:22; 20:30, 31). Jesus responds by quoting from Psalm 8:3.

21:18-22 The withered fig tree

This strange story may have evolved from the parable of the fig tree in Luke 13:6-9. Fruitful figs and vines are a symbol of peace and prosperity

sea,' it will be done. ²²Whatever you ask for in prayer with faith, you will receive."

The Authority of Jesus Questioned. ²³When he had come into the temple area, the chief priests and the elders of the people approached him as he was teaching and said, "By what authority are you doing these things? And who gave you this authority?" ²⁴Jesus said to them in reply, "I shall ask you one question, and if you answer it

for me, then I shall tell you by what authority I do these things. ²⁵Where was John's baptism from? Was it of heavenly or of human origin?" They discussed this among themselves and said, "If we say 'Of heavenly origin,' he will say to us, 'Then why did you not believe him?' ²⁶But if we say, 'Of human origin,' we fear the crowd, for they all regard John as a prophet." ²⁷So they said to Jesus in reply, "We do not know." He himself said to them, "Neither shall I

(1 Kgs 4:25), and Matthew frequently uses the metaphor "bear fruit" to speak of doing righteous deeds (cf. 3:8; 7:15-20; 12:33-37; 13:23; 21:19, 33-43). In the Matthean setting, there are strong eschatological overtones from chapter 21 forward. The time has arrived when there must be evidence of "good fruit," or else there will be destruction of the temple and condemnation of those who lead people astray (see also Jer 8:13; Hos 9:10, 16). The last two verses shift emphasis, so that the story becomes one about the power of faith (see also 7:7-11; cf. 6:30; 8:25, 26; 14:30, 31; 16:8; 17:20, where Jesus chides the disciples for their lack of faith). Jesus does not promise that the object of every prayerful request will be granted; rather, he assures believers that when they pray with faith in God's gracious goodness, God will always be with them (1:23; 28:20). God's power is at work in believers, even when they confront the most insurmountable obstacles.

21:23-27 The authority of Jesus

Throughout Matthew's Gospel, Jesus is portrayed as the authoritative teacher whom many people follow but whom the leaders reject. Now there are open confrontations between Jesus and the religious authorities. The chief priests and elders (v. 23) are the leading opponents in the passion narrative (the Pharisees drop out of view after chapter 23). Their trap backfires, and they themselves are trapped by Jesus' question. Three parables follow, the first two of which indirectly answer the question about the source of Jesus' authority.

21:28-32 Saying and doing

The technique Jesus uses is like that of Nathan (2 Sam 12:1-12), whereby the hearers are asked for their opinion and end by pronouncing

tell you by what authority I do these things.

The Parable of the Two Sons. ◁ ²⁸"What is your opinion? A man had two sons. He came to the first and said, 'Son, go out and work in the vineyard today.' ²⁹He said in reply, 'I will not,' but afterwards he changed his mind and went. ³⁰The man came to the other son and gave the same order. He said in reply, 'Yes, sir,' but did not go. ³¹Which of the two did his father's will?" They answered, "The first." Jesus said to them, "Amen, I say to you, tax collectors and prostitutes are entering the ◁ kingdom of God before you. ³²When

John came to you in the way of righteousness, you did not believe him; but tax collectors and prostitutes did. Yet even when you saw that, you did not later change your minds and believe him.

The Parable of the Tenants. ³³"Hear ▷ another parable. There was a landowner who planted a vineyard, put a hedge around it, dug a wine press in it, and built a tower. Then he leased it to tenants and went on a journey. ³⁴When ▷ vintage time drew near, he sent his servants to the tenants to obtain his produce. ³⁵But the tenants seized the servants and one they beat, another

judgment on themselves. The parable seems a simple one at first. Both children (the word in verse 28 is *teknon*, "child," not *huios*, "son") fall short of the ideal. But the one who appeared to *do* the father's will was the first.

However, in a culture that highly prizes honor, the answer is not so clear. In some manuscript variants of this parable, the one who gives the correct answer is the second child. The first child shamed the father publicly, a worse fault than failing to carry through on one's word. At 7:21-27 Jesus insisted to his disciples that saying *and* doing are necessary; now he directs this message to religious authorities who do not practice what they preach (23:3). Verses 31-32 contrast the leaders, who should most exemplify righteousness, with those who are thought least able to do so. But there is still time for the leaders to repent. Those who initially refuse to say yes to Jesus and do the will of God can still change their minds.

21:33-43 Treacherous tenants

Matthew reworks Mark's version (12:1-12), making the parable more allegorical and more pointedly christological. It is a familiar story, echoing Isaiah 5, but with a new ending. In Isaiah 5 Yahweh decides to destroy the vineyard after disappointment over the yield of sour grapes from Israel, the carefully cultivated vine. In Jesus' parable the tenants are destroyed; the vineyard remains and is entrusted to others. The eschatological time (*kairos*, v. 34) demands that fruit be evident now (see 21:18-22). The repeated sending of the servants (vv. 34-39) is like God's repeated sending

they killed, and a third they stoned. ³⁶Again he sent other servants, more numerous than the first ones, but they treated them in the same way. ³⁷Finally, he sent his son to them, thinking, 'They will respect my son.' ³⁸But when the tenants saw the son, they said to one another, 'This is the heir. Come, let us kill him and acquire his inheritance.' ³⁹They seized him, threw him out of the vineyard, and killed him. ⁴⁰What will the owner of the vineyard do to those tenants when he comes?" ⁴¹They answered him, "He will put those wretched men to a wretched death and lease his vineyard to other tenants who will give him the produce at the proper times." ⁴²Jesus said to them, "Did you never read in the scriptures:

'The stone that the builders rejected
has become the cornerstone;
by the Lord has this been done,
and it is wonderful in our eyes'?

⁴³Therefore, I say to you, the kingdom of God will be taken away from you and given to a people that will produce its fruit. [⁴⁴The one who falls on this stone will be dashed to pieces; and it

---

of the prophets to Israel. Prophets were called "servants" of God (Jer 7:25; 25:4; Amos 3:7; Zech 1:6), and their fates match those in the parable (see Jer 20:2; 26:20-23; 2 Chr 24:21).

The sequence of actions in verse 39 corresponds to the details of Jesus' passion. He is seized (26:50), taken outside the city limits (27:31-32), and then killed (27:35). The murderous plans of the tenants in the vineyard match the intent of the chief priests and Pharisees (21:46; 22:15) toward Jesus. The chief priests and elders pronounce their own self-condemnation (v. 41), but the future tense verbs show that the possibility is yet open so the Jewish leaders can still change their minds (as also 21:29, 32). They could still be among those "other tenants" to whom the vineyard will be entrusted.

Jesus' question in verse 42 (see also 12:3, 5; 19:4; 21:16) underscores the conflict between Jesus' interpretation of Scripture and that of the opposing religious leaders. The quotation from Psalm 118 in verse 42 recalls God's unlikely choice of David as king, the prototype for the Messiah, and points toward the leadership of the new Israel as coming from those rejected as unimportant. At the conclusion (vv. 45-46) the chief priests and Pharisees clearly understand the parable (cf. 13:51), but instead of heeding Jesus' invitation, they plot his arrest.

22:1-14 Dressed for the feast

This is the third of three parables that Jesus addresses to the religious leaders in Jerusalem after they challenged his authority (21:23-27). The parable is highly allegorized and has a number of unrealistic details. The

will crush anyone on whom it falls.]" [45]When the chief priests and the Pharisees heard his parables, they knew that he was speaking about them. [46]And although they were attempting to arrest him, they feared the crowds, for they regarded him as a prophet.

22 **The Parable of the Wedding Feast.** [1]Jesus again in reply spoke to them in parables, saying, [2]"The kingdom of heaven may be likened to a king who gave a wedding feast for his son. [3]He dispatched his servants to summon the invited guests to the feast, but they refused to come. [4]A second time he sent other servants, saying, 'Tell those invited: "Behold, I have prepared my banquet, my calves and fattened cattle are killed, and everything is ready; come to the feast."' [5]Some ignored the invitation and went away, one to his farm, another to his business. [6]The rest laid hold of his servants, mistreated them, and killed them. [7]The king was enraged and sent his troops, destroyed those murderers, and burned their city. [8]Then he said to his servants, 'The feast is ready, but those who were invited were not worthy to come. [9]Go out, therefore, into the main roads and invite to the feast whomever you find.' [10]The servants went out into the streets and gathered all they found, bad and good alike, and the hall was filled with guests. [11]But when the king came in to meet the guests he saw a man there not dressed in a wedding garment. [12]He said to him, 'My friend, how is it that you came in here without a wedding garment?' But he was reduced to silence. [13]Then the king said to his attendants, 'Bind his hands and feet, and cast him into the darkness outside, where there will be wailing and grinding of teeth.' [14]Many are invited, but few are chosen."

image of a wedding banquet recalls Matthew 9:15, where Jesus was likened to a groom, whose presence demands feasting, not fasting. This metaphor is frequently used in the Scriptures to signify God's abundant care, both now and at the end time (e.g., Isa 25:6-10; 55:1-3). The repeated invitation is reminiscent of the multiple envoys in 21:33-46 and has an echo of Lady Wisdom inviting all to her banquet (Prov 9:5). The custom of a double invitation (see Esth 5:8; 6:14) allowed the potential guest to find out who the other guests were and whether all was being arranged appropriately. It also gave them time to decide if they would be able to reciprocate. The time lapse also allowed the host to determine the amount of food needed.

Unlike Luke 14:15-24, there are no detailed excuses offered by the invitees. Their mistreatment and killing of the king's servants (vv. 5-6) and the king's enraged response (v. 7), are allegorical allusions to the killing of John the Baptist and the prophets and the destruction of Jerusalem in A.D. 70. The king's retaliation can be expected in an honor-and-shame system,

Paying Taxes to the Emperor. [15]Then the Pharisees went off and plotted how they might entrap him in speech. [16]They sent their disciples to him, with the Herodians, saying, "Teacher, we know that you are a truthful man and that you teach the way of God in accordance with the truth. And you are not concerned with anyone's opinion, for you do not regard a person's status. [17]Tell us, then, what is your opinion: Is it lawful to pay the census tax to Caesar or not?" [18]Knowing their malice, Jesus said, "Why are you testing me, you hypocrites? [19]Show me the coin that pays the census tax." Then they handed him the Roman coin. [20]He said to them, "Whose image is this and whose inscription?" [21]They replied, "Caesar's." At that he said to them, "Then repay to Caesar what belongs to Caesar and to God what belongs to God." [22]When they heard this they were amazed, and leaving him they went away.

in which one responds in kind to an affront. But his second response (vv. 8-10) is shocking. In a first-century Mediterranean world likes eat with likes, since eating together signifies sharing of values and of social position. The king sends his servants out to the places where the main road cuts through the city boundary, going out to the countryside (v. 10). This is where the poorer people lived, while the elite (5 to 10 percent of the population) lived in the center of the city. Like the parables in 13:24-30, 47-50, both "good" and "bad" are gathered in, and then there is sorting out.

The last scene (vv. 11-14) is entirely unrealistic but highlights Matthew's ethical concern: one must be ready at all times for the end-time banquet, clothed with good deeds (similarly Rom 13:14; Gal 3:27; Col 3:12). More is required of a disciple than initial acceptance of the invitation to be a "friend of God and prophets" (Wis 7:27). See also 20:13, where the grumbler is called "friend," as is Judas at the moment of betrayal (26:50). In the Matthean narrative context, the parable is a warning to the religious leaders who are offered repeated invitations to accept Jesus. The seriousness of their refusal is painted with vivid metaphors: they will be cast into the outer darkness (so also 8:12; 25:30), where there is weeping and gnashing of teeth (8:12, 13:42, 50; 24:51; 25:30). The proverbial saying in verse 14 does not entirely capture the meaning of the parable. The focus is on how those who are expected to respond to the invitation (the religious leaders) refuse, while the unexpected invitees (the socially marginal) have accepted.

22:15-22 Taxes to Caesar

This is the first of four more controversies between Jesus and the religious leaders. Their flattering words (v. 16) are true but insincere, as they

The Question about the Resurrection. ²³On that day Sadducees approached him, saying that there is no resurrection. They put this question to him, ²⁴saying, "Teacher, Moses said, 'If a man dies without children, his brother shall marry his wife and raise up descendants for his brother.' ²⁵Now there were seven brothers among us. The first married and died and, having no descendants, left his wife to his brother. ²⁶The same happened with the second and the third, through all seven. ²⁷Finally the woman died. ²⁸Now at the resurrection, of the seven, whose wife will she be? For they all had been married to her." ²⁹Jesus said to them in reply, "You are misled because you do not know the scriptures or the power of God. ³⁰At the resurrection they neither marry nor are given in marriage but are like the angels in heaven. ³¹And concerning the resurrection of the dead, have you not read what was said to you by God, ³²'I am the God of Abraham, the God of Isaac, and the God of Jacob'? He is not the God of the dead but of the living." ³³When the crowds

proceed to lay a deliberate trap (v. 15). The question is a sticky one. Since the Roman occupation of Palestine in 63 B.C., Jews were obliged to pay tribute, or a head tax, in Roman coinage, on each man, woman, and slave. If Jesus opposes this payment, he would be advocating revolt against Rome. If he advocates payment, then he would be seen as a collaborator with the enemy. Jesus sees the malice and hypocrisy of his questioners, who have set this trap (v. 18). His clever response can be understood in one of three ways: (1) one should pay nothing to Caesar because everything belongs to God (Lev 25:23); (2) one should pay the emperor because he is God's representative (as Rom 13:1-7; 1 Pet 2:13-17); (3) one can pay Caesar but recognize that his authority is relative and that loyalty to God takes precedence. The last is the most likely meaning. As in 17:24-27, Jesus advises paying the tax, but this is not a vote of support for the occupying power. The amazed response (v. 22) of the Pharisees' disciples (see also 8:27; 9:33; 15:31; 21:20) underscores Jesus' skill in outwitting his opponents.

22:23-33 The question of resurrection

In this second controversy the Sadducees pose a question that derides belief in the resurrection. Ideas about the afterlife were diverse in Jesus' day. The notion of resurrection of the dead first appears in the book of Daniel (12:2), written in the second century B.C., and was accepted by the Pharisees but not the Sadducees (see Acts 23:6). The situation posed by the Sadducees, citing Deuteronomy 25:5-10, is absurd (although see Tobit 3:8; 6:14, where Sarah, the daughter of Raguel, outlives seven husbands). Like the previous question, it is set up to try to make Jesus contradict his

heard this, they were astonished at his teaching.

The Greatest Commandment.
◄ ³⁴When the Pharisees heard that he had silenced the Sadducees, they gathered together, ³⁵and one of them [a scholar of the law] tested him by asking,

³⁶"Teacher, which commandment in the ►
law is the greatest?" ³⁷He said to him, ►
"You shall love the Lord, your God, with all your heart, with all your soul, and with all your mind. ³⁸This is the greatest and the first commandment. ³⁹The second is like it: You shall love

own teaching or the Scriptures. It is a Bible battle in which Jesus emerges as authoritative teacher.

Jesus responds by accusing his opponents of not knowing the Scriptures or the power of God. He cites Exodus 3:6, 15-16 to argue that Israel's ancestors, who were physically dead at the time that God spoke to Moses, continued to be in relationship with God, and so they were in some sense among the living. Jesus also asserts that the Sadducees do not understand the nature of resurrection. By God's power new life will be created that is continuous in some way with the life we have known, yet it will be brought to fullness in ways we do not yet know.

22:34-40 The greatest commandment

In Mark's account (12:28-34; cf. Luke 10:25), the scribe's question is sincere, but in Matthew it leads to another controversy. The Pharisees gather together (v. 34), signaling a plot against Jesus (see 2:4; 22:41; 26:3; 27:17, 27; 28:12; possibly this also alludes to Ps 2:2). The question they pose is meant to test him (see also 22:15). All commandments are important; all must be kept. The query is not whether some laws can be disregarded, but whether Jesus, like some teachers, would sum up the Torah in a simple statement, as did Rabbi Hillel: "What is hateful to you do not do to your neighbor" (*b. Šabb.* 31a).

Jesus summarizes the whole of the Law in two commandments (see also 7:12). The first, the *Shema* (Deut 6:4-9), was recited twice a day by Jews. It enjoins love of God with one's whole heart, soul, and strength. The heart (*kardia*), was considered the seat of all emotions, the soul (*psychē*), the center of vitality and consciousness, and strength (*ischys*) denotes power or might. The second command, love of neighbor, is from the Holiness Code (Lev 19:18), which asserts that love of God is manifest in love toward the neighbor. The modern Western notion of the necessity of self-love would have been a foreign concept to people of the biblical world. They did not understand themselves in individualistic terms, but rather as enmeshed in a particular family, clan, and religious group.

your neighbor as yourself. [40]The whole law and the prophets depend on these two commandments."

The Question about David's Son.
[41]While the Pharisees were gathered together, Jesus questioned them, [42]saying, "What is your opinion about the Messiah? Whose son is he?" They replied, "David's." [43]He said to them, "How, then, does David, inspired by the Spirit, call him 'lord,' saying:

[44]"The Lord said to my lord,
"Sit at my right hand
until I place your enemies under
your feet"'?

[45]If David calls him 'lord,' how can he be his son?" [46]No one was able to answer him a word, nor from that day on did anyone dare to ask him any more questions.

23 Denunciation of the Scribes and Pharisees. [1]Then Jesus spoke to

---

Dependent on others for their sense of self-identity, love of self and love of others are inseparable.

22:41-46 David's son

In the fourth and final controversy, Jesus is the one who initiates the questioning. Again, the debate centers on the correct interpretation of Scripture. The text in question is Psalm 110:1, a coronation psalm, in which God assures the new king of special honor (sitting at the right hand) and a vanquishing of his enemies (making them subservient, "under your feet"). The speaker in the psalm is David, who says that the "Lord" (*kyrios*), meaning Yahweh, is speaking to "my lord" (*kyrios*), meaning the new king.

Jesus stumps his opponents by asking that if David, inspired by the Spirit, calls the new king (here equated with the messiah) "lord," then he must be more than simply his son. The notion that the messiah would be a "son of David" is found in Isaiah 11:1, 10; Jeremiah 23:5. Although this is a favorite Matthean title for Jesus (1:1; 9:27; 12:23; 15:22; 20:30, 31; 21:9, 15), "Son of David" is not adequate to express all that Jesus is. This text brings together several important christological titles intimating that Jesus is also Messiah, Son of God, and Lord. The silence of Jesus' opponents indicates a victory for him. There will be no further exchanges with the leaders until the passion narrative, as he speaks now only with the crowds and his disciples.

23:1-12 Warning against hypocrisy

The whole of this chapter is a stinging denunciation by Jesus of the scribes and Pharisees, who have been cast as his opponents throughout the Gospel. Matthew expands a brief critique of scribes from Mark 12:38-40, weaving in material from Q and Luke 11:37-52. In the New Testament,

the crowds and to his disciples, ²saying, "The scribes and the Pharisees have taken their seat on the chair of Moses. ³Therefore, do and observe all things whatsoever they tell you, but do not follow their example. For they preach but they do not practice. ⁴They tie up heavy burdens [hard to carry] and lay them on people's shoulders, but they will not lift a finger to move them. ⁵All their works are performed to be seen. They widen their phylacteries and lengthen their tassels. ⁶They love places of honor at banquets, seats of honor in synagogues, ⁷greetings in marketplaces, and the salutation 'Rabbi.' ⁸As for you, do not be called 'Rabbi.' You have but one teacher, and you are all brothers. ⁹Call no one on earth your father; you have but one Father in heaven. ¹⁰Do not be called 'Master'; you have but one master, the Messiah. ¹¹The greatest among you must be your servant. ¹²Whoever exalts himself will be humbled; but whoever humbles himself will be exalted.

¹³"Woe to you, scribes and Pharisees, you hypocrites. You lock the kingdom of heaven before human beings.

scribes are religious leaders who are learned in Torah. Pharisees, lay religious leaders, differed from Sadducees in their belief in resurrection (see 22:23-33) and in oral interpretation of the Law. The excoriating tone of Jesus' rebuke reflects the vehemence of the conflict between the Christians of Matthew's community, who were predominantly Jewish, and the Jews of emerging rabbinic Judaism.

Jesus takes on the role of a prophet, much like Amos (5:18-20; 6:1-7) or Isaiah (5:8-10, 11-14) , who uses the classic "woe" form to denounce the wrongdoing of a group of his own people, with the intent to turn them from evil and toward right relation with God. Jesus' words are a warning to the crowds and his disciples (v. 1) not to follow the hypocritical practices of these leaders, who do not practice what they teach (v. 3). In contrast to Jesus, whose burden is light (11:30), they lay heavy loads on people's shoulders (v. 4). They make their phylacteries and fringes noticeable to all (v. 5). (Phylacteries are leather boxes containing the parchment texts such as Exodus 13:1-16; Deuteronomy 6:4-9; 11:13-22, which are strapped to the forehead and arm during morning prayer.) Wearing "tassels" or "fringes" at the corners of the outer garments reminds a Jew to observe all God's commands (Num 15:38-39; Deut 22:12; Matt 9:20; 14:36). Jesus also criticizes the leaders' love of places of honor and deferential titles (vv. 6-10)—only he and God are to bear these titles. Like many other reform movements, there was an impulse in early Christianity toward egalitarianism and status reversal (vv. 11-12; see also 18:1-4; 19:13-15; 20:20-28).

You do not enter yourselves, nor do you allow entrance to those trying to enter.[14]

15"Woe to you, scribes and Pharisees, you hypocrites. You traverse sea and land to make one convert, and when that happens you make him a child of Gehenna twice as much as yourselves.

16"Woe to you, blind guides, who say, 'If one swears by the temple, it means nothing, but if one swears by the gold of the temple, one is obligated.' 17Blind fools, which is greater, the gold, or the temple that made the gold sacred? 18And you say, 'If one swears by the altar, it means nothing, but if one swears by the gift on the altar, one is obligated.' 19You blind ones, which is greater, the gift, or the altar that makes the gift sacred? 20One who swears by the altar swears by it and all that is upon it; 21one who swears by the temple swears by it and by him who dwells in it; 22one who swears by heaven swears by the throne of God and by him who is seated on it.

23"Woe to you, scribes and Pharisees, you hypocrites. You pay tithes of mint and dill and cummin, and have neglected the weightier things of the law: judgment and mercy and fidelity. [But] these you should have done, without neglecting the others. 24Blind guides, who strain out the gnat and swallow the camel!

25"Woe to you, scribes and Pharisees, you hypocrites. You cleanse the

23:13-36 Seven woes

In the seven woes that ensue, the religious leaders are repeatedly called "hypocrites"—a term that originally referred to an actor, one who put on a mask to assume another personage. In the first woe (vv. 13-14), Jesus denounces the scribes and Pharisees not only because they fail to enter into God's realm themselves but, worse yet, they block the way for others. The image of unlocking and locking the way to heaven recalls Matthew 16:19, where Peter is given the keys to God's realm. For Matthew's community, Peter and the leaders of the emergent Christian community are the authorities to be heeded rather than those of the synagogue.

The second woe (v. 15) is an accusation that the Gentile converts to Pharisaism are twice as zealous and twice as misguided as their teachers. Jesus warns that in the end they will be "child[ren] of Gehenna" rather than "children of God" (e.g., Matt 5:9, cf. 45). The name "Gehenna" derives from "The Valley (*gē*) of Hinnom," which runs south-southwest of Jerusalem. It represented the place of fiery judgment, because it was there that fires of the cult of Molech and later, smoldering refuse, were located.

In the third woe (vv. 16-22), Jesus critiques the meaningless distinctions the Pharisees invented in their oath-taking. In Jesus' world, binding obligations were set not by contracts but with one's word, by public

outside of cup and dish, but inside they are full of plunder and self-indulgence. [26]Blind Pharisee, cleanse first the inside of the cup, so that the outside also may be clean.

[27]"Woe to you, scribes and Pharisees, you hypocrites. You are like whitewashed tombs, which appear beautiful on the outside, but inside are full of dead men's bones and every kind of filth. [28]Even so, on the outside you appear righteous, but inside you are filled with hypocrisy and evildoing.

[29]"Woe to you, scribes and Pharisees, you hypocrites. You build the tombs of the prophets and adorn the memorials of the righteous, [30]and you say, 'If we had lived in the days of our ancestors, we would not have joined them in shedding the prophets' blood.'

---

swearing. For the most serious agreements, God's name would be invoked. But devout Jews objected to speaking God's name aloud. Just as Matthew substituted "the reign of heaven" for "the reign of God" (see 3:2), so Pharisees would swear on the gold or the gifts of the temple, objects associated with God, as a way to avoid saying the divine name. Jesus says that these fine distinctions are useless; the effect is the same. See Matthew 5:33-37 on not taking oaths at all.

In the fourth woe (vv. 23-24), Jesus accuses the leaders of not being able to distinguish between what is important and what is not. The texts on tithing (see Lev 27:30-33; Num 18:21-32; Deut 14:22-29) prescribe giving one-tenth of one's produce, flocks, wine, grain, and oil to support the temple, the Levites, and the poor. They do not mention herbs, such as mint, dill, and cumin. Jesus teaches his disciples that their observance of the Law must go beyond what is written (Matt 5:21-48), but the point is to arrive at more complete harmony with God and all that God has created (5:20, 48). The Pharisees, by contrast, engage in intensified practices of keeping the Law that lead them away from deeds of justice, mercy, and faith. Thus they become "blind guides," not seeing the way clearly themselves and leading others onto a destructive path. The outrageousness of their practice is captured in the hyperbole "swallow the camel."

The fifth woe (vv. 25-26) contrasts outer practices with inner dispositions. Jesus uses a strong term, *harpagēs*, "pillage, plunder," to speak of the corrupt inner state of the scribes and Pharisees, who misuse their power to exploit others. He also accuses them of *akrasia*, "lack of self-control" and "want of power" (see v. 25). The reference is to sexual activity or intemperance in general. By contrast, the interior disposition Jesus has taught his disciples is purity of heart (5:8), the ability to forgive from the heart (18:35), and love of God with all one's heart (22:37).

117

[31]Thus you bear witness against yourselves that you are the children of those who murdered the prophets; [32]now fill up what your ancestors measured out! [33]You serpents, you brood of vipers, how can you flee from the judgment of Gehenna? [34]Therefore, behold, I send to you prophets and wise men and scribes; some of them you will kill and crucify, some of them you will scourge in your synagogues and pursue from town to town, [35]so that there may come upon you all the righteous blood shed upon earth, from the righteous blood of Abel to the blood of Zechariah, the son of Barachiah, whom you murdered be-

The sixth woe (vv. 27-28) continues in the same vein as the fifth. The Pharisees and scribes present a lovely exterior, seeming to be in right relation with God and others, while their interior disposition is rotten with hypocrisy and evildoing. Like white-washed sepulchers, they hide putrid decay within. White-washing sepulchers made them easily visible, so that Jews could avoid contact with them and thus maintain ritual purity (see Lev 21:1, 11).

In the seventh and last woe (vv. 29-36), the Pharisees and scribes pretend to honor the prophets and righteous ancestors with decorated monuments and protest that had they been alive earlier, they would never have done what their ancestors did to the prophets. In truth, Jesus says, they are no different from their forebears. They will kill the prophet Jesus just as their ancestors rid themselves of the pesky prophets who denounced their unrighteousness. They show themselves to be not children of God but children of Gehenna (v. 15) and children of murderers (v. 31), linked to all the innocent blood shed from Abel to Zechariah, the first victim of murder in the Bible (Gen 4:8) to the last. There is some confusion about the identity of Zechariah. The Old Testament prophet Zechariah was the son of Barachiah (Zech 1:1), but as far as we know, he was not murdered "between the sanctuary and the altar" (v. 35), as was Zechariah, son of Jehoiada (2 Chr 24:20-22).

The theme of responsibility for innocent blood is an important one in the passion narrative as Judas tries to return the blood money (27:4), Pilate tries to wash himself of guilt for Jesus' blood (27:24), and the people say to Pilate, "His blood be on us and on our children" (27:25). At the Last Supper Jesus offers to his disciples his "blood of the covenant" (26:28) for the forgiveness of sins.

23:37-39 Lament over Jerusalem
The tone shifts from vehement denunciation of the leaders to profound sadness for the city which destroys God's messengers and which,

tween the sanctuary and the altar. [36]Amen, I say to you, all these things will come upon this generation.

The Lament over Jerusalem. [37]"Jerusalem, Jerusalem, you who kill the prophets and stone those sent to you, how many times I yearned to gather your children together, as a hen gathers her young under her wings, but you were unwilling! [38]Behold, your house will be abandoned, desolate. [39]I tell you, you will not see me again until you say, 'Blessed is he who comes in the name of the Lord.'"

24 **The Destruction of the Temple Foretold.** [1]Jesus left the temple area and was going away, when his disciples approached him to point out the temple buildings. [2]He said to them in reply, "You see all these things, do you not? Amen, I say to you, there will not be left here a stone upon another stone that will not be thrown down."

The Beginning of Calamities. [3]As he was sitting on the Mount of Olives, the disciples approached him privately and said, "Tell us, when will this happen, and what sign will there be of your

---

by Matthew's day, lies in ruins. The poignant image of a mother bird yearning to gather her rebellious young under her wings is a common metaphor in the Scriptures for God's loving care (Deut 32:11; Ruth 2:12; Pss 17:8; 36:7; 57:1; 61:4; Luke 13:34-35). But like a mother who never abandons even the most wayward child, Jesus, quoting Psalm 118:26, holds out the promise that they will see him again when they can receive him as did the disciples when he first entered Jerusalem (21:9).

The denunciations and woes in this chapter must always be read in the context of a bitter internal family dispute between the Jewish Christians and Jews who did not join them in Matthew's day. Jesus is a prophet admonishing his own leaders and inviting them to a change of heart. His words still sound a warning against hypocrisy to any religious leaders.

24:1–25:46 The apocalyptic discourse

Jesus has been teaching his disciples and warning and disputing with other religious leaders since 21:23. He now leaves the temple area and directs his instruction only to his disciples (24:1, 3). He speaks of the calamities that presage the coming of the Human One (24:1-33) and tells three parables (24:45–25:30) that emphasize the need for watchfulness. The parable of the final judgment (25:31-46) brings this last block of teaching to a climax.

24:1-14 The beginning of the end

The tension between Jesus and the temple leadership has been mounting. He has performed a prophetic action of purification in the temple (21:12-17), he has engaged in debates with the temple leadership

coming, and of the end of the age?" ⁴Jesus said to them in reply, "See that no one deceives you. ⁵For many will come in my name, saying, 'I am the Messiah,' and they will deceive many. ⁶You will hear of wars and reports of wars; see that you are not alarmed, for these things must happen, but it will not yet be the end. ⁷Nation will rise against nation, and kingdom against kingdom; there will be famines and earthquakes from place to place. ⁸All these are the beginning of the labor pains. ⁹Then they will hand you over to persecution, and they will kill you. You will be hated by all nations because of my name. ¹⁰And then many will be led into sin; they will betray and hate one another. ¹¹Many false prophets will arise and deceive many; ¹²and because of the increase of evildoing, the love of many will grow cold. ¹³But the one who perseveres to the end will be saved. ¹⁴And this gospel of the kingdom will be preached throughout the world as a witness to all nations, and then the end will come.

The Great Tribulation. ¹⁵"When you see the desolating abomination

(21:23–22:46), and he has warned his disciples about their hypocrisy (23:1-36). This comes to a head as Jesus now predicts the very destruction of the temple (24:1-2), an occurrence that Jeremiah (7:1-15) associated with the messianic age. In Matthew's day this has already occurred. At his interrogation before the Jewish leaders, false witnesses accuse Jesus of making threats against the temple (26:61) and passers-by deride him about this in the crucifixion scene (27:40).

Jesus then speaks about the signs of the end times. He is seated, as authoritative teacher (see also 5:10; 15:29), on the Mount of Olives, the place associated with the final judgment (Zech 14:4). As in the parable discourse (13:10-17), Jesus' disciples receive private instruction. He paints a picture of massive chaos and destruction, with a proliferation of false messiahs, wars, famines, earthquakes, persecution, hatred because of Jesus' name, sin, betrayal, deception, lawlessness, and loss of fervor. Strife comes both from within and from without.

In almost every age people see these signs and wonder if they herald the end. A similar theme is found in the mission discourse (10:16-25, 34-39), where Jesus also assured his disciples not to fear anything because of God's constant care for them (10:26-33). Here as well, Jesus tells them that if they persevere to the end, they will be saved (v. 13). These birthpangs (v. 8) are the prelude to new life. For Matthew, this end is not imminent—the Gospel must first be preached throughout the whole world (see also 28:16-20).

24:15-31 Signs of the coming of the Human One

There will be unmistakable signs when the end actually does come. It will be as evident as lightning across the sky (v. 27) or vultures circling

spoken of through Daniel the prophet standing in the holy place (let the reader understand), [16]then those in Judea must flee to the mountains, [17]a person on the housetop must not go down to get things out of his house, [18]a person in the field must not return to get his cloak. [19]Woe to pregnant women and nursing mothers in those days. [20]Pray that your flight not be in winter or on the sabbath, [21]for at that time there will be great tribulation, such as has not been since the beginning of the world until now, nor ever will be. [22]And if those days had not been shortened, no one would be saved; but for the sake of the elect they will be shortened. [23]If anyone says to you then, 'Look, here is the Messiah!' or, 'There he is!' do not believe it. [24]False messiahs and false prophets will arise, and they will perform signs and wonders so great as to deceive, if that were possible, even the elect. [25]Behold, I have told it to you beforehand. [26]So if they say to you, 'He is in the desert,' do not go out there; if they say, 'He is in the inner rooms,' do not believe it. [27]For just as lightning comes from the east and is seen as far as the west, so will the coming of the Son of Man be. [28]Wherever the corpse is, there the vultures will gather.

The Coming of the Son of Man. [29]"Immediately after the tribulation of those days,

the sun will be darkened,
and the moon will not give its
light,
and the stars will fall from the sky,
and the powers of the heavens
will be shaken.

[30]And then the sign of the Son of Man will appear in heaven, and all the tribes of the earth will mourn, and they will see the Son of Man coming upon the clouds of heaven with power and great glory. [31]And he will send out his angels with a

---

over a corpse (v. 28). One sign will be like the one spoken of by Daniel, the "desolating abomination" (v. 15; Dan 9:27; 11:31; 12:11). In Daniel this referred to the statue that Antiochus IV Epiphanes placed in the temple in 167 B.C., which sparked the Maccabean revolt. Still fresh in the memories of Matthew's community is that the emperor Caligula threatened a similar action in A.D. 40.

A future event of this caliber will signal the end. This is a time when immediate flight is the response to the danger (as in 2:12-13, 10:23). As is so often the case, it is mothers and children who are the most adversely affected. The disciples are to pray that it not happen at a time when the hardship would be intensified, such as winter or the sabbath. Fleeing on the sabbath (v. 20) may have drawn attention to the community and put them at risk. Or it could be a cause of division if some thought flight would break sabbath observance.

trumpet blast, and they will gather his elect from the four winds, from one end of the heavens to the other.

The Lesson of the Fig Tree. ³²"Learn a lesson from the fig tree. When its branch becomes tender and sprouts leaves, you know that summer is near. ³³In the same way, when you see all these things, know that he is near, at the gates. ³⁴Amen, I say to you, this generation will not pass away until all these things have taken place. ³⁵Heaven and earth will pass away, but my words will not pass away.

The Unknown Day and Hour. ³⁶"But of that day and hour no one knows, neither the angels of heaven, nor the Son, but the Father alone. ³⁷For as it was in the days of Noah, so it will be at the coming of the Son of Man. ³⁸In [those] days before the flood, they were eating and drinking, marrying and giving in marriage, up to the day that Noah entered the ark. ³⁹They did not know until the flood came and carried them all away. So will it be [also] at the coming of the Son of Man. ⁴⁰Two men will be out in the field; one will be taken, and one will be left. ⁴¹Two women will be grinding at the mill; one will be taken, and one will be left. ⁴²Therefore, stay awake! For you do not

---

Cosmic signs (as in Isa 13:10; 34:4; Ezek 32:7; Joel 2:10, 31; 3:4; 4:15; Amos 8:9; Hag 2:6, 21) preface the final sign before the coming of the Human One (see comments at 8:20). Why mourning (v. 30) will accompany this sign is not clear—is it because of the tribulations or because people are repenting? The motif of God gathering in the elect at the end time is a common one (Deut 30:3-4; Isa 11:11-12; Ezek 37:21; 39:27-29; Zech 2:6-12).

24:32-51 Parables of watchfulness

A series of parables and figurative sayings exhorts disciples to watchfulness. The fig tree (vv. 32-35), which is different from other trees in Palestine (most are evergreens), sheds all its leaves in winter. Just as its budding is a sign of the arrival of summer, the signs in the previous verses alert disciples to the coming of the Human One. There is a tension between verse 34, which assures that the end is imminent, and verse 14, which asserts that the Gospel first has to be preached to the whole world. Disciples need to be both ready and steadfast, trusting in Jesus' words, which will never pass away (similarly the Torah, 5:18). The timing of the end is unpredictable, so disciples need to stay awake (see also 26:38, 40, 41).

While the previous verses emphasize watchfulness for the coming of the master, the parable of the faithful servant (vv. 45-51) exhorts disciples to vigilance in day-to-day tasks that must be fulfilled in the in-between time. One of these is the daily distribution of food (v. 45). This detail may be an allusion to the difficulties in the early church over food and eating, such as conflicts over Gentile and Jewish Christians eating together (Gal

know on which day your Lord will come. ⁴³Be sure of this: if the master of the house had known the hour of night when the thief was coming, he would have stayed awake and not let his house be broken into. ⁴⁴So too, you also must be prepared, for at an hour you do not expect, the Son of Man will come.

The Faithful or the Unfaithful Servant. ⁴⁵"Who, then, is the faithful and prudent servant, whom the master has put in charge of his household to distribute to them their food at the proper time? ⁴⁶Blessed is that servant whom his master on his arrival finds doing so. ⁴⁷Amen, I say to you, he will put him in charge of all his property. ⁴⁸But if that wicked servant says to himself, 'My master is long delayed,' ⁴⁹and begins to beat his fellow servants, and

eat and drink with drunkards, ⁵⁰the servant's master will come on an unexpected day and at an unknown hour ⁵¹and will punish him severely and assign him a place with the hypocrites, where there will be wailing and grinding of teeth.

25 **The Parable of the Ten Virgins.** ¹"Then the kingdom of heaven will be like ten virgins who took their lamps and went out to meet the bridegroom. ²Five of them were foolish and five were wise. ³The foolish ones, when taking their lamps, brought no oil with them, ⁴but the wise brought flasks of oil with their lamps. ⁵Since the bridegroom was long delayed, they all became drowsy and fell asleep. ⁶At midnight, there was a cry, 'Behold, the bridegroom! Come out to meet him!' ⁷Then all those virgins got up and

---

2:11-14) or having people of differing social status at the same table (22:1-14). Alternatively, giving food may be understood as a metaphor for teaching (so 1 Cor 3:2; John 6:25-33), and the parable as an exhortation to leaders to exercise their teaching ministry well. The warning to those who gorge themselves on the resources meant for the community is dire; such a one will be dismembered (*dichotomēsei*, literally, "cut in two," v. 51) as a condemned person.

25:1-13 Ready maidens

A second parable advising preparedness for the coming of the Human One casts Jesus in the role of a bridegroom (as 9:15; see Isa 54:5; Jer 31:32; Hos 2:16, where Yahweh is the bridegroom of Israel). In Jesus' day, weddings took place in two stages. First was the betrothal ceremony at the home of the father of the bride, at which the groom presented the marriage contract and the bride price to his future father-in-law. The bride continued to live in her father's house until the second step, when she would move to the home of her husband, about a year later. This is the stage depicted in the parable. The maidens are waiting while the groom and the bride's father hammer out the final negotiations. Upon reaching a

trimmed their lamps. [8]The foolish ones said to the wise, 'Give us some of your oil, for our lamps are going out.' [9]But the wise ones replied, 'No, for there may not be enough for us and you. Go instead to the merchants and buy some for yourselves.' [10]While they went off to buy it, the bridegroom came and those who were ready went into the wedding feast with him. Then the door was locked. [11]Afterwards the other virgins came and said, 'Lord, Lord, open the door for us!' [12]But he said in reply, 'Amen, I say to you, I do not know you.' [13]Therefore, stay awake, for you know neither the day nor the hour.

The Parable of the Talents. [14]"It will be as when a man who was going on a journey called in his servants and entrusted his possessions to them. [15]To one he gave five talents; to another, two; to a third, one—to each according to his ability. Then he went away. Immediately [16]the one who received five talents went and traded with them, and made another five. [17]Likewise, the one who received two made another two. [18]But the man who received one went off and dug a hole in the ground and buried his master's money. [19]After a long time the master of those servants came back and settled accounts with them. [20]The one who had received five talents came forward bringing the additional five. He said, 'Master, you gave me five talents. See, I have made five

---

final agreement, the wedding party would go in procession to the house of the groom, where the feasting would commence.

The waiting women are friends of the groom; the bride is never mentioned in the story. The word *parthenos* refers to a virgin, a young woman of marriageable age (twelve or in her early teens). The contrast between wise and foolish recalls the builders in 7:24-27. It is not clear whether the women are carrying torches (the usual connotation of *lampades*) wrapped with oil-soaked rags or hand-held oil lamps with lighted wicks. Matthew 5:14-16 provides a clue to interpreting why the women cannot share their oil. There light is equated with good deeds that are visible to others and lead to praise of God. Similarly, at Matthew 7:24-27 the wise are those who hear and act on Jesus' words. Just so, the wise maidens in this parable are those who have faithfully prepared for the end time. No one can supply this preparation for another. One is either ready or not at the eschatological moment.

25:14-30 Investing talents

This parable is often interpreted as an exhortation to use all one's God-given gifts to the full. However, the Greek word *talanton* has no other connotation than a monetary unit or weight measurement. In the parable it denotes a very large sum of money. What the parable depicts are two ser-

more.' [21]His master said to him, 'Well done, my good and faithful servant. Since you were faithful in small matters, I will give you great responsibilities. Come, share your master's joy.' [22][Then] the one who had received two talents also came forward and said, 'Master, you gave me two talents. See, I have made two more.' [23]His master said to him, 'Well done, my good and faithful servant. Since you were faithful in small matters, I will give you great responsibilities. Come, share your master's joy.' [24]Then the one who had received the one talent came forward and said, 'Master, I knew you were a demanding person, harvesting where you did not plant and gathering where you did not scatter; [25]so out of fear I went off and buried your talent in the ground. Here it is back.' [26]His master said to him in reply, 'You wicked, lazy servant! So you knew that I harvest where I did not plant and gather where I did not scatter? [27]Should you not then have put my money in the bank so that I could have got it back with interest on my return? [28]Now then! Take the talent from him and give it to the one with ten. [29]For to everyone who has, more will be given and he will grow rich; but from the one who has not, even what he has will be taken away. [30]And throw this useless servant into the darkness outside, where there will be wailing and grinding of teeth.'

---

vants who invest and double the money with which they are entrusted, which wins them their master's approval, a share in his joy, and further responsibility. The third servant, by contrast, buries the money, which was considered the best way of safeguarding valuables in antiquity. Yet he earns harsh punishment from the master.

Key to understanding the parable is that Jesus did not live in a capitalist system, where it was thought that wealth can be increased by investment. Rather, people had a notion of limited good: there is only so much wealth, and any increase to one person takes away from another. The aim in life for a peasant was to have enough to take care of his family. Anyone amassing large amounts for himself would be seen as greedy and wicked. In the parable, then, if the master is not a figure for God, it is the third servant who is the honorable one—only he has refused to collaborate with his master in his unfettered greed. The parable warns rich people to stop exploiting those who are poor, and it encourages poor people to take courageous measures to expose greed for the sin that it is. The last verse is sobering, depicting what can happen to those who oppose the rich and powerful. It can encourage disciples to find ways to stand together as they confront unjust systems. There is still opportunity, since the end time has not yet arrived.

The Judgment of the Nations. ³¹"When the Son of Man comes in his glory, and all the angels with him, he will sit upon his glorious throne, ³²and all the nations will be assembled before him. And he will separate them one from another, as a shepherd separates the sheep from the goats. ³³He will place the sheep on his right and the goats on his left. ³⁴Then the king will say to those on his right, 'Come, you who are blessed by my Father. Inherit the kingdom prepared for you from the foundation of the world. ³⁵For I was hungry and you gave me food, I was thirsty and you gave me drink, a stranger and you welcomed me, ³⁶naked and you clothed me, ill and you cared for me, in prison and you visited me.' ³⁷Then the righteous will answer him and say, 'Lord, when did we see you hungry and feed you, or thirsty and give you drink? ³⁸When did we see you a stranger and welcome you, or naked and clothe you? ³⁹When did we see you ill or in prison, and visit you?' ⁴⁰And the king will say to them in reply, 'Amen, I say to you, whatever you did for one of these least brothers of mine, you did for me.' ⁴¹Then he will say to those on his left, 'Depart from me, you accursed, into the eternal fire prepared for the devil and his angels. ⁴²For I was hungry and you gave me no food, I was thirsty and you gave me no drink, ⁴³a stranger and you gave me no welcome, naked and you gave me no clothing, ill and in prison, and you did not care for me.' ⁴⁴Then they will answer and say, 'Lord, when did we see you hungry or thirsty or a stranger or naked or ill or in prison, and not minister to your needs?' ⁴⁵He will answer them, 'Amen, I say to you, what you did not do for one of these least ones, you did not do for me.' ⁴⁶And these will go off to eternal punishment, but the righteous to eternal life."

25:31-46 Final judgment

This is the last of Matthew's parables and is unique to this Gospel. The time of judgment has arrived as the Human One comes in his glory (v. 31). This scene is intimately linked with 28:16-20, where Jesus instructs his followers to make disciples of all nations (*panta ta ethnē*, 28:19), a command that this parable presumes has been fulfilled. All the nations (v. 32) are now assembled to render account. The reason why the sheep are separated from the goats is not clear. Both were very valuable. Nor is there any evidence that after pasturing them together during the daytime, a shepherd would separate the two at night. (See 3:12; 13:24-30, 47-50; 24:40-41; 25:1-13 for other images of end-time separation.) Since most people were right-handed and developed greater strength and skill with this hand, the right side came to symbolize favor, blessing, and honor.

The image of Jesus shifts from shepherd to king (v. 34; see 2:2; 21:5). And, like Moses, who laid out before the Israelites the choice of blessing or curse (Deut 11:26), Jesus separates those "blessed by my Father" (v. 34)

VII. The Passion and Resurrection

26
The Conspiracy against Jesus. [1]When Jesus finished all these words, he said to his disciples, [2]"You know that in two days' time it will be Passover, and the Son of Man will be handed over to be crucified." [3]Then the chief priests and the elders of the people assembled in the palace of the high priest, who was called Caiaphas, [4]and they consulted together to arrest Jesus by treachery and put him to death. [5]But they said, "Not during the festival, that there may not be a riot among the people."

The Anointing at Bethany. [6]Now when Jesus was in Bethany in the house of Simon the leper, [7]a woman came up to him with an alabaster jar of costly perfumed oil, and poured it on his head while he was reclining at table. [8]When the disciples saw this, they were indignant and said, "Why this waste? [9]It could have been sold for much, and the money given to the poor." [10]Since Jesus knew this, he said to them, "Why do you make trouble for the woman? She has done a good thing for me. [11]The poor you will always have with you; but you will not always have me. [12]In pouring this

---

from those "accursed" (v. 41). This is not predestined; rather, God's invitation goes out to all (5:45; 13:3-9), and the choice to accept or reject it rests with each. For those who accept the invitation, which is visible in their deeds, blessing and inheritance in God's realm await.

In light of the saying at 24:14, it is likely that Matthew envisions the completion of the great commission (28:16-20); all people, including Israel, Gentiles, and Christians, have heard the Gospel and are now judged according to their deeds. The "least brothers" (v. 40) and "least ones" (v. 45) most likely refer to other Christians rather than to just any person in need. See 11:11; 18:6, 14, where "little ones" and "least" refer to vulnerable members of the Christian community, and 10:41-42, where Jesus promises the reward of a righteous person for those who receive the needy ones sent out on mission. The basis of judgment, then, is how one receives Jesus through his followers who proclaim the Gospel (see 10:40).

26:1–27:66 The passion and resurrection

Matthew's usual formula at the end of a block of teaching, "When Jesus finished . . ." (26:1, as also 7:28; 11:1; 13:53; 19:1), marks the transition to the passion narrative. There is also an echo of Deuteronomy 32:45, where Moses finished his instruction to Israel and then prepared for his death. In these final scenes Matthew follows Mark closely, while adding his own unique touches. Jesus is portrayed as knowing what will happen and as being in control of the events. As Matthew is wont to do, he interprets each action as fulfilling the Scriptures.

perfumed oil upon my body, she did it to prepare me for burial. ¹³Amen, I say to you, wherever this gospel is proclaimed in the whole world, what she has done will be spoken of, in memory of her."

The Betrayal by Judas. ¹⁴Then one of the Twelve, who was called Judas Iscariot, went to the chief priests ¹⁵and said, "What are you willing to give me if I hand him over to you?" They paid him thirty pieces of silver, ¹⁶and from that time on he looked for an opportunity to hand him over.

Preparations for the Passover. ¹⁷On ▶ the first day of the Feast of Unleavened Bread, the disciples approached Jesus and said, "Where do you want us to prepare for you to eat the Passover?" ¹⁸He said, "Go into the city to a certain man and tell him, 'The teacher says, "My appointed time draws near; in your house I shall celebrate the Pass-

26:1-16 Preparation for death:
Treacherous plotting and prophetic anointing

For the fourth and last time (16:21; 17:22-23; 20:18-19), Jesus predicts his death. The prime movers are the chief priests and elders (v. 3), along with the high priest, Caiaphas (v. 3), who held office from A.D. 18 to 36. The Pharisees and scribes, who have been Jesus' opponents up to this point in the narrative, drop out of view until 27:62. The people are still basically favorable toward Jesus (v. 5).

In strong contrast to the leaders' treachery is the action of an anonymous woman who anoints Jesus in the home of Simon the leper. This takes place in Bethany, a village just east of Jerusalem, over the Mount of Olives. In the Gospel of John this is identified as the home of Martha, Mary, and Lazarus (John 11:1–12:12). By anointing Jesus' head, the woman takes on the role of priest and prophet. She both prepares Jesus for burial (v. 12) and commissions him as messianic king (see Sam 16:12-13; 1 Kgs 1:39). Jesus affirms her action, over the objection of the disciples. There is no question of a lack of concern for the poor by Jesus (see 5:3, 42; 6:2-4, 24; 19:21; 25:31-46); rather, the issue is the timing and the woman's recognition of Jesus' fate. She embodies the understanding and loyalty of the women disciples who, in contrast to the others (26:56), remain to see the crucifixion (27:55-56), keep vigil at the tomb (27:61), and are the first to encounter the risen Christ (28:1-10). Her pouring of oil on Jesus' head (v. 6) prefigures Jesus' pouring out of his blood for all (v. 28). While her action is remembered (v. 13), her identity is not.

In strong contrast is the act of Judas (vv. 14-16), who negotiates with the chief priests to hand Jesus over to them. No motive is given (cf. John 12:6). Once again Matthew interprets this deed through Scripture. Thirty

over with my disciples."'" ¹⁹The disciples then did as Jesus had ordered, and prepared the Passover.

The Betrayer. ²⁰When it was evening, he reclined at table with the Twelve. ²¹And while they were eating, he said, "Amen, I say to you, one of you will betray me." ²²Deeply distressed at this, they began to say to him one after another, "Surely it is not I, Lord?" ²³He said in reply, "He who has dipped his hand into the dish with me is the one who will betray me. ²⁴The Son of Man indeed goes, as it is written of him, but woe to that man by whom the Son of Man is betrayed. It would be better for that man if he had never been born." ²⁵Then Judas, his betrayer, said in reply, "Surely it is not I, Rabbi?" He answered, "You have said so."

The Lord's Supper. ²⁶While they were eating, Jesus took bread, said the blessing, broke it, and giving it to his disciples said, "Take and eat; this is my

---

pieces of silver is the worth of a slave (Exod 21:32). But probably the allusion is to Zechariah 11:12-13, where this is the amount of a shepherd's wage, which Judas casts back into the treasury (see 27:3-10).

26:17-35 The Last Supper

As the woman prepared Jesus for his passion, so now Jesus prepares his disciples. In the first scene (vv. 17-19), the disciples approach (*prosēlthon*, the reverential stance also of the woman in v. 7; also 4:3, 11; 5:1; 8:2) Jesus and ask about Passover preparations. Jesus' reply has an apocalyptic nuance, as Matthew uses both *kairos*, "appointed time" (8:29; cf. 13:30; 16:3; 21:34), and *engiken*, "draws near" (cf. 3:2; 4:17; 10:7; 21:34; 24:32-33) in reference to the end time.

The meal begins with a notation that Jesus is with his disciples (v. 20). His words and actions interpret for his intimate followers ("Twelve" is symbolic for all, as also 10:1-4) how he is still present with them ("Emmanuel," 1:23; cf. 28:20), even when his earthly life ends. Tragic predictions of betrayal (vv. 20-25) and denial (vv. 31-35) by his closest disciples frame Jesus' eucharistic words and actions (vv. 26-30). In verses 20-25 there is a contrast between the obedience of Jesus (v. 24) and the disobedience of Judas, who calls Jesus "Rabbi" (vv. 25 and 49), after Jesus has instructed his disciples not to use that address (23:8). The allusion to Psalm 41:10 in verse 23 captures the anguish of betrayal by an intimate friend. Typically, Matthew signals the dire consequences of not acting justly with a pronunciation of woe (as 11:21; 18:7; 23:13, 15, 16, 23, 25, 27, 29; 24:19). Unique to Matthew is the personal exchange between Judas and Jesus (v. 25; also 26:49-50). Jesus' enigmatic "you have said so" is the same response he gives to the high priest (26:64) and to Pilate (27:11).

body." [27]Then he took a cup, gave thanks, and gave it to them, saying, "Drink from it, all of you, [28]for this is my blood of the covenant, which will be shed on behalf of many for the forgiveness of sins. [29]I tell you, from now on I shall not drink this fruit of the vine until the day when I drink it with you new in the kingdom of my Father." [30]Then, after singing a hymn, they went out to the Mount of Olives.

Peter's Denial Foretold. [31]Then Jesus said to them, "This night all of you will have your faith in me shaken, for it is written:

'I will strike the shepherd,
and the sheep of the flock will
be dispersed';

[32]but after I have been raised up, I shall go before you to Galilee." [33]Peter said to him in reply, "Though all may have their faith in you shaken, mine will never be." [34]Jesus said to him, "Amen, I say to you, this very night before the cock crows, you will deny me three times." [35]Peter said to him, "Even though I should have to die with you, I will not deny you." And all the disciples spoke likewise.

The Agony in the Garden. [36]Then Jesus came with them to a place called Gethsemane, and he said to his disciples, "Sit here while I go over there and pray." [37]He took along Peter and the two sons of Zebedee, and began to feel sorrow and distress. [38]Then he said

---

The institution of the Eucharist (vv. 26-29) is the core and climax of this section. Jesus' gift of self in the form of bread is reminiscent of the feedings of the multitudes (14:13-21; 15:32-39) and of the similar actions by Elijah and Elisha (1 Kgs 17: 8-16; 2 Kgs 4:42-44), as well as of God's provision of manna in the desert for Israel (Exod 16). The cup in which all participate symbolizes both his death (see 20:22; 26:39, 42) and a ratification of a renewed life in covenantal fidelity. Blood, as the symbol of life (Deut 12:23), was sprinkled by Moses on the altar and on the people (Exod 24:8) to seal the covenant.

A unique element in Matthew's account is the interpretation that this action is "on behalf of many, for the forgiveness of sins" (v. 28). This is an allusion to the servant in Isaiah 53:4-12 (see also 12:17-21; 20:28). The "many" *(pollōn)* is a Semitic expression meaning "all"; no one is excluded from the saving effects of Jesus' death (see 1:21). Forgiveness is possible even for those who hand Jesus over to death. The gift of bread and wine also sounds an eschatological note, as the messianic banquet of Isaiah 25:6-9 is in view. Jesus assures his disciples that while the intimacy of eating and drinking together, which they shared during his earthly life, is ending, they will yet experience this with him in the realm of God (v. 29).

The scene shifts to the Mount of Olives (v. 31; see 24:3), where jubilant singing (Psalms 114–118 are sung at the conclusion of the Passover meal)

to them, "My soul is sorrowful even to death. Remain here and keep watch with me." [39]He advanced a little and fell prostrate in prayer, saying, "My Father, if it is possible, let this cup pass from me; yet, not as I will, but as you will." [40]When he returned to his disciples he found them asleep. He said to Peter, "So you could not keep watch with me for one hour? [41]Watch and pray that you may not undergo the test. The spirit is willing, but the flesh is weak." [42]Withdrawing a second time, he prayed again, "My Father, if it is not possible that this cup pass without my drinking it, your will be done!" [43]Then he returned once more and found them asleep, for they could not keep their eyes open. [44]He left them and withdrew again and prayed a third time, saying the same thing again. [45]Then he returned to his disciples and said to them, "Are you still sleeping and taking your rest? Behold, the hour is at hand when the Son of Man is to be handed over to sinners. [46]Get up, let us go. Look, my betrayer is at hand."

The Betrayal and Arrest of Jesus. [47]While he was still speaking, Judas, one of the Twelve, arrived, accompanied by a large crowd, with swords and clubs, who had come from the chief

---

gives way to a sober prediction by Jesus that all the disciples will have their faith shaken (*skandalizesthai*, literally, to find Jesus a "stumbling block" or "obstacle." See also 11:6; 13:57; 15:12). A quotation from Zechariah 13:7 that speaks of the disintegration of the community is accompanied by a promise of its renewal. Galilee is the place where Jesus first gathered disciples (4:18-22) and commissioned them (10:1-42) and where he appears to them for the last time, sending them to the whole world (28:16-20). Peter, representative of the whole (see 16:16-23), boasts that this will never happen (vv. 33-35). The irony is strong, as in the next scene the disciples sleep instead of keeping watch (vv. 36-46) and flee (v. 56), while the women disciples stay the course (27:55-56, 61; 28:1-10).

26:36-46 Prayer at Gethsemane

Arriving at Gethsemane (meaning "olive press") with his disciples (v. 36; see 26:20), Jesus separates himself from them to pray, taking along Peter and the sons of Zebedee, namely, James and John. These three were among the first called and sent (4:18-22; 10:2) and were privileged witnesses at the Transfiguration (17:1-8). They are also singled out as the ones who struggled most to understand Jesus' passion (16:22; 20:20-23). The separation of Jesus from the rest of the disciples may be an allusion to Genesis 22:5, where Abraham tells his servants to stay back while he and Isaac pray. While Abraham is exemplary in his faithfulness, he misinterprets what action God desires. Jesus is both faithful to God and understands

priests and the elders of the people. ⁴⁸His betrayer had arranged a sign with them, saying, "The man I shall kiss is the one; arrest him." ⁴⁹Immediately he went over to Jesus and said, "Hail, Rabbi!" and he kissed him. ⁵⁰Jesus answered him, "Friend, do what you have come for." Then stepping forward they laid hands on Jesus and arrested him. ⁵¹And behold, one of those who accompanied Jesus put his hand to his sword, drew it, and struck the high priest's servant, cutting off his ear. ⁵²Then Jesus said to him, "Put your sword back into its sheath, for all who take the sword will perish by the sword. ⁵³Do you think that I cannot call upon my Father and he will not provide me at this moment with more than twelve legions of angels? ⁵⁴But then how would the scriptures be fulfilled which say that it must come to pass in this way?" ⁵⁵At that hour Jesus said to the crowds, "Have you come out as against a robber, with swords and clubs to seize me? Day after day I sat teaching in the temple area, yet you did not arrest me. ⁵⁶But all this has come to pass that the writings of the prophets may be fulfilled." Then all the disciples left him and fled.

Jesus before the Sanhedrin. ⁵⁷Those who had arrested Jesus led him away to Caiaphas the high priest, where the scribes and the elders were assembled. ⁵⁸Peter was following him at a distance as far as the high priest's courtyard, and going inside he sat down with the ser-

---

what action will bring liberation for his people. For him there will be no rescuing angel (26:53).

Three times Jesus implores God (on the metaphor of "Father" for God, see the comments on 6:5-15) to let the cup (a metaphor for death; see 20:22; 26:27) pass from him without drinking it. His grief is extreme (quoting lament psalms 42:4-5; 43:5 at v. 38), and his struggle is real. Jesus is not a puppet in the hand of God. His death is not inevitable. He wrestles with the final choice to proceed with handing over his life.

Jesus' faithfulness in seeking and following God's direction stands in contrast with the frailty of his disciples. They fail to keep watch (see chs. 24–25) and do not pray, as Jesus had instructed (v. 41 and 6:13), to be delivered from the test *(peirasmos)*—both the present crisis and the eschatological trial. Yet they will be restored and empowered by the risen Christ (28:7, 16-20). The final scenes of intimacy between Jesus and his followers began with Jesus noting at the supper that his appointed hour was at hand (26:18). They now close with his declaration that both the hour and the one handing him over are at hand (vv. 45-46).

26:47-56 Jesus' arrest

Jesus' words are immediately fulfilled with the arrival of Judas and a large, armed crowd, who come on the authority of the chief priests and

vants to see the outcome. [59]The chief priests and the entire Sanhedrin kept trying to obtain false testimony against Jesus in order to put him to death, [60]but they found none, though many false witnesses came forward. Finally two came forward [61]who stated, "This man said, 'I can destroy the temple of God and within three days rebuild it.' " [62]The high priest rose and addressed him, "Have you no answer? What are these men testifying against you?" [63]But Jesus was silent. Then the high priest said to him, "I order you to tell us under oath before the living God whether you are the Messiah, the Son of God." [64]Jesus said to him in reply, "You have said so. But I tell you:

> From now on you will see 'the Son of Man
> seated at the right hand of the Power'
> and 'coming on the clouds of heaven.' "

elders. With so many people in the city for the feast, Judas has pre-arranged a signal so that there will be no confusion. A kiss, normally given by a disciple to a teacher as a sign of respect, turns treacherous. And as at the Last Supper (26:25), Judas addresses Jesus as Rabbi (v. 49), against Jesus' instructions (23:8). The tone of Jesus' response (v. 50) is not clear. It can be understood as an ironic question, "Friend, why are you here?" (KJV) or an instruction that emphasizes Jesus' control of the scene: "Friend, do what you have come for" (NAB). Or, by addressing Judas as "friend," he reminds him of their intimate relationship and holds out to him the possibility of forgiveness, recalling that Judas has partaken in the cup of his blood that is shed for forgiveness of sins (26:28).

A desperate attempt on the part of a disciple to halt the arrest (v. 51) serves to underscore once again a lack of understanding. Jesus has taught his followers not to counter violence with violence (5:38-48), which he re-inforces here with a pronouncement unique to Matthew: "all who take the sword will perish by the sword" (v. 52; similarly Rev 13:10). Moreover, Jesus withstands the temptation to call upon angelic rescuers (v. 53, as at 4:6). As always, Matthew explains that all these seemingly incomprehensible events happen to fulfill the Scriptures (v. 54, 56). The fallibility of the disciples culminates with their desertion and fleeing (v. 56; but see 27:55-56, 61; 28:1-10, where the Galilean women continue to follow and serve).

26:57-68 Interrogation before the Sanhedrin

The arresting party brings Jesus to the high priest, scribes, and elders (the Pharisees have dropped from view in the passion narrative and only reappear at 27:62). The mention of Peter (v. 58) prepares for the next scene, in which he denies Jesus (vv. 69-75). The Jewish leaders do not have

⁶⁵Then the high priest tore his robes and said, "He has blasphemed! What further need have we of witnesses? You have now heard the blasphemy; ⁶⁶what is your opinion?" They said in reply, "He deserves to die!" ⁶⁷Then they spat in his face and struck him, while some slapped him, ⁶⁸saying, "Prophesy for us, Messiah: who is it that struck you?"

Peter's Denial of Jesus. ⁶⁹Now Peter was sitting outside in the courtyard. One of the maids came over to him and said, "You too were with Jesus the Galilean." ⁷⁰But he denied it in front of everyone, saying, "I do not know what you are talking about!" ⁷¹As he went out to the gate, another girl saw him and said to those who were there, "This

---

authority to put a person to death (John 18:31). While Matthew gives the scene the aura of a trial, it is more a strategy session to prepare the case they will present to Pilate. In Christian tradition, the blame for Jesus' death increasingly has been taken off the Romans and put on the Jewish leaders. Matthew paints the Jewish leaders as vile, seeking *false* testimony (v. 59; cf. Mark 14:55) against Jesus.

Two witnesses are necessary for a death sentence (Deut 17:6). The accusation that Jesus said he can destroy the temple and rebuild it (v. 61) is both false and ironically correct. Although he performed a prophetic act in judgment on the temple (21:1-17) and remarked about its coming destruction (24:2), he did not say that he himself would destroy it. But since destruction and restoration of the temple were thought to be a sign of the messianic age, the accusation is actually true. Jesus' initial silence toward the high priest (v. 63) recalls that of the servant in Isaiah 53:7. At 27:40 the charge will be made again by passers-by reviling the crucified Jesus.

The high priest shifts the focus, demanding that Jesus respond under oath to the charge that he is Messiah, Son of God (v. 64). That Jesus is Messiah has been affirmed from the opening line of the Gospel (1:1, 17, 18; 2:4; 11:2; 16:16; 22:42; 23:10). "Son of God" underscores his unique relationship with God (2:15; 3:17; 11:25-27; 17:5), his healing power (8:29), and his authority (see 14:33; 16:20, where the two titles occur in tandem). Jesus had taught his disciples not to take oaths (7:33-37). He replies to the high priest with the same enigmatic phrase, "You have said so" (v. 64), that he had said to Judas (26:25) and to Pilate (27:11). His further response underscores his identity as the coming Human One. Blending Psalm 110:1 and Daniel 7:13, he moves the discussion to an eschatological plane. At this the high priest accuses Jesus of blasphemy, that is, abusing the divine name or insulting God (v. 65), an offense the leaders deem worthy of death (v. 66). They themselves begin to abuse Jesus (cf. Mark 14:65, where it is an

man was with Jesus the Nazorean." ⁷²Again he denied it with an oath, "I do not know the man!" ⁷³A little later the bystanders came over and said to Peter, "Surely you too are one of them; even your speech gives you away." ⁷⁴At that he began to curse and to swear, "I do not know the man." And immediately a cock crowed. ⁷⁵Then Peter remembered the word that Jesus had spoken: "Before the cock crows you will deny me three times." He went out and began to weep bitterly.

27 Jesus before Pilate. ¹When it was morning, all the chief priests and the elders of the people took counsel against Jesus to put him to death. ²They bound him, led him away, and handed him over to Pilate, the governor.

The Death of Judas. ³Then Judas, his betrayer, seeing that Jesus had been condemned, deeply regretted what he

---

anonymous "some") and mock his identity as prophet and Messiah (vv. 67-68), an element unique to Matthew.

26:69-75 Peter denies Jesus

The utter failure of Peter is not unexpected; Jesus has warned that this will happen (26:31-35). Peter has been in the lead as one of the first disciples called (4:18-22) and was a privileged witness at the Transfiguration (17:1-8). He was the spokesperson for the disciples in declaring Jesus "messiah" (16:16), and the one to whom Jesus entrusted the "keys to the kingdom of heaven" (16:19). But he has also been the prime example of a disciple who struggles to understand and fails miserably (16:22-23; 26:33-35). Not once but three times he denies being with Jesus, and he does so with an oath (see 5:33-37, where Jesus forbids oath-taking). Matthew adds that Peter makes the denial "in front of everyone" (v. 70; cf. 5:16; 10:32-33). This is the last mention of Peter in Matthew's Gospel. Presumably his bitter tears (v. 75) are tears of repentance, and he is among the disciples to whom the women announce the good news (28:7-10) and among those who are commissioned to preach to all the nations (28:16).

27:1-2 The council hands Jesus over

After a night of interrogation and abuse, the chief priests and elders fulfill what Jesus had predicted at 20:18-19. They hand Jesus over (*paradidōmi*, 10:4; 26:15, 25; 27:3, 18, 26) to the Roman governor, Pontius Pilate, who ruled from A.D. 26 to 36.

27:3-10 The death of Judas

Seeing Jesus condemned prompts a change of heart in Judas. Ordinarily the verb *metanoein* is used for repentance, whereas here it is *metamelētheis*, "deeply regretted" (v. 3). But it is likely that Judas' words in

had done. He returned the thirty pieces of silver to the chief priests and elders, [4]saying, "I have sinned in betraying innocent blood." They said, "What is that to us? Look to it yourself." [5]Flinging the money into the temple, he departed and went off and hanged himself. [6]The chief priests gathered up the money, but said, "It is not lawful to deposit this in the temple treasury, for it is the price of blood." [7]After consultation, they used it to buy the potter's field as a burial place for foreigners. [8]That is why that field even today is called the Field of Blood. [9]Then was fulfilled what had been said through Jeremiah the prophet, "And they took the thirty pieces of silver, the value of a man with a price on his head, a price set by some of the Israelites, [10]and they paid it out for the potter's field just as the Lord had commanded me."

Jesus Questioned by Pilate. [11]Now Jesus stood before the governor, and he questioned him, "Are you the king of the Jews?" Jesus said, "You say so." [12]And when he was accused by the chief priests and elders, he made no answer. [13]Then Pilate said to him, "Do you not hear how many things they are testifying against you?" [14]But he did not answer him one word, so that the governor was greatly amazed.

The Sentence of Death. [15]Now on the occasion of the feast the governor was accustomed to release to the crowd one prisoner whom they wished. [16]And at that time they had a notorious pris-

---

verse 4 indicate true repentance and not simply regret. Judas, like the leaders Jesus warned in 23:35-36, is responsible for shedding innocent blood. (See 27:24, where Pilate will try to make himself innocent of Jesus' blood.) The leaders dissociate themselves from Judas' attempt to return the money (see 27:24 for Pilate's use of the same phrase, "Look to it yourselves"). In desperation, Judas flings the money into the temple and tragically ends his life. A rather different version is found in Acts 1:15-20. The quotation in verses 9-10 interpreting the purchase of the "Field of Blood" is actually an adaptation of Zechariah 11:12-13, although Matthew attributes it to Jeremiah. Perhaps Matthew makes the association because of a similarity with the slaughter of the innocents (2:17-18), interpreted with Jeremiah 31:15. Or Matthew may mean to recall Jesus' critique of the temple and its leadership (21:13, quoting Jer 7:11). Alternatively, he may be alluding to the story of the potter's field in Jeremiah 18–19.

27:11-14 Trial before Pilate

Resuming the action begun at verse 2, Matthew now tells of the interrogation by the Roman governor. His question is different from that of the Jewish authorities and concerns Jesus' kingship. Once again Jesus answers enigmatically, "You say so" (v. 11; see 26:64), and then remains silent when the chief priests and elders testify against him (as also 26:63).

oner called [Jesus] Barabbas. [17]So when they had assembled, Pilate said to them, "Which one do you want me to release to you, [Jesus] Barabbas, or Jesus called Messiah?" [18]For he knew that it was out of envy that they had handed him over. [19]While he was still seated on the bench, his wife sent him a message, "Have nothing to do with that righteous man. I suffered much in a dream today because of him." [20]The chief priests and the elders persuaded the crowds to ask for Barabbas but to destroy Jesus. [21]The governor said to them in reply, "Which of the two do you want me to release to you?" They answered, "Barabbas!" [22]Pilate said to them, "Then what shall I do with Jesus called Messiah?" They all said, "Let him be crucified!" [23]But he said, "Why? What evil has he done?" They only shouted the louder, "Let him be crucified!" [24]When Pilate saw that he was not succeeding at all, but that a riot was breaking out instead, he took water and washed his hands in the sight of the crowd, saying, "I am innocent of this man's blood. Look to it yourselves." [25]And the whole people said in reply, "His blood be upon us and upon our children." [26]Then he released Barabbas to them, but after he had Jesus scourged, he handed him over to be crucified.

Jesus' silence is evocative again of the servant of Isaiah 53:7, whose appearance caused amazement (Isa 52:14-15; v. 14).

27:15-26 Choice of Barabbas

Beyond the Gospel references, there is no other evidence of a custom of releasing a prisoner at Passover. The choice, according to Matthew, is between Jesus Barabbas and "Jesus called Messiah" (v. 17). Matthew heightens the notoriety of the former (v. 16) and names envy as the motive for handing Jesus over (v. 18). Three other unique elements in Matthew serve to shift the blame away from Pilate and onto the Jewish leaders. The first is the dream of Pilate's wife, who urges her husband to "have nothing to do with that righteous man" (v. 19). In the opening chapters, dreams are the means by which Joseph, a "righteous man" (1:19), learns God's desire and by what actions he is to preserve the life of Jesus and his mother (1:20; 2:13, 19, 22). A second element found only in Matthew is Pilate's handwashing (v. 24), a futile attempt to declare his own innocence and to dissociate himself from Jesus' death (similarly the chief priests with Judas, 27:4). A third unique feature of the Matthean account is the climactic cry of the whole people, "His blood be upon us and upon our children" (v. 25).

Until this point the crowds have been basically favorable toward Jesus. Now they demand his crucifixion (vv. 22, 23), and the people as a whole (*laos*, as at 1:21) take upon themselves the responsibility for his

Mockery by the Soldiers. [27]Then the soldiers of the governor took Jesus inside the praetorium and gathered the whole cohort around him. [28]They stripped off his clothes and threw a scarlet military cloak about him. [29]Weaving a crown out of thorns, they placed it on his head, and a reed in his right hand. And kneeling before him, they mocked him, saying, "Hail, King of the Jews!" [30]They spat upon him and took the reed and kept striking him on the head. [31]And when they had mocked him, they stripped him of the cloak, dressed him in his own clothes, and led him off to crucify him.

---

blood (v. 25; see Lev 20:9-16; Josh 2:19-20; 2 Sam 1:16; 14:9; Jer 51:35). This verse has been interpreted as a curse upon all Jewish people for all time. This is a grave misinterpretation that Christians have a serious obligation to counter (see the Vatican II document *Nostra Aetate* 4). In the context of Matthew's Gospel, "the whole people" refers to those who opposed Jesus during his lifetime as well as Jewish opponents of the early Christian community. Verse 25 reflects the inner family conflict and the struggle of Jesus' disciples to understand why all Jews did not follow Jesus (similarly Matthew 13; Romans 9–11). Matthew sees a connection between the rejection of Jesus and the events that unfold in the decades following Jesus' death ("upon our children"), particularly the destruction of the temple. The scene concludes with Pilate releasing Barabbas, having Jesus scourged to weaken him, and handing him over (*paradidōmi*,10:4; 20:18; 26:15, 25; 27:2, 3, 18, 26) for the last time to the soldiers to crucify him.

27:27-31 Mockery by the soldiers

Just as the interrogation before the chief priests and elders ended with them abusing Jesus (26:67-68), so the Roman trial concludes with abuse by the soldiers of the governor inside the praetorium, the governor's official residence. A cohort consisted of six hundred men; in verse 27 it likely refers to simply a large group of soldiers. These would have been local men employed by the Romans. They mock Jesus' kingship, arraying him in scarlet, with a pseudo-crown and scepter. In Mark 15:17 the robe is purple, a color worn by royalty and the rich (see, e.g., Luke 16:19), but Matthew's detail is more realistic. Roman soldiers wore red cloaks; they simply adorn Jesus in one of their own. The crown of thorns was not so much to inflict pain as to imitate that of an emperor with its rays. The acclamation (v. 29) simulates the greeting toward the emperor, "Ave, Caesar!" The derisive mockery turns to physical abuse (v. 30) and ends with Jesus being led to crucifixion.

The Way of the Cross. ³²As they were going out, they met a Cyrenian named Simon; this man they pressed into service to carry his cross.

The Crucifixion. ³³And when they came to a place called Golgotha (which means Place of the Skull), ³⁴they gave Jesus wine to drink mixed with gall. But when he had tasted it, he refused to drink. ³⁵After they had crucified him, they divided his garments by casting lots; ³⁶then they sat down and kept watch over him there. ³⁷And they placed over his head the written charge against him: This is Jesus, the King of the Jews. ³⁸Two revolutionaries were crucified with him, one on his right and the other on his left. ³⁹Those passing by reviled him, shaking their heads ⁴⁰and saying, "You who would destroy the temple and rebuild it in three days, save yourself, if you are the Son of God, [and] come down from the cross!" ⁴¹Likewise the chief priests with the scribes and elders mocked him and said, ⁴²"He saved others; he cannot save himself. So he is the king of Israel! Let him come down from the cross now, and we will believe in him. ⁴³He trusted in God; let him deliver him now if he wants him. For he said, 'I am the Son of God.'" ⁴⁴The revolutionaries who were crucified with him also kept abusing him in the same way.

27:32 Simon of Cyrene

On the way to the site of crucifixion, Simon of Cyrene (a North African city in present-day Libya) is pressed into service to help Jesus carry the cross. Likely he was visiting Jerusalem for the Passover feast. While Jesus has said that those who wish to be his follower must take up their cross (16:24), discipleship motifs are not entirely clear in this scene, especially since Simon is forced into carrying the crossbeam. At the same time, the presence of this Simon is a poignant reminder of the absence of Simon Peter, who has struggled to accept the fact that Jesus would die (16:21-23), then declared he would follow Jesus to the death (26:33-35), but has fled (26:56) and denied that he was ever with Jesus (26:69-75).

27:33-44 Crucifixion and mockery

The place of crucifixion, Golgotha, "Place of the Skull," gets its name either because the hill is skull-shaped or because of the executions that took place there. It was customary to give the condemned person a drink mixed with a narcotic to ease the pain. Matthew makes it wine mixed with gall, so that the action corresponds to what is said in Psalm 69:21.

No details are narrated about the crucifixion itself (v. 35). Matthew's readers are well familiar with what other contemporary writers describe as the most cruel and painful of all punishments. It was used on slaves, violent criminals, and political rebels. Carried out in a public place, it was

The Death of Jesus. ⁴⁵From noon onward, darkness came over the whole land until three in the afternoon. ⁴⁶And about three o'clock Jesus cried out in a loud voice, *"Eli, Eli, lema sabachthani?"* which means, "My God, my God, why have you forsaken me?" ⁴⁷Some of the bystanders who heard it said, "This one is calling for Elijah." ⁴⁸Immediately one of them ran to get a sponge; he soaked it in wine, and putting it on a reed, gave it to him to drink. ⁴⁹But the rest said, "Wait, let us see if Elijah comes to save him." ⁵⁰But Jesus cried out again in a loud voice, and gave up his spirit. ⁵¹And behold, the veil of the sanctuary was torn in two from top to bottom. The earth quaked, rocks were split, ⁵²tombs were opened, and the bodies of many saints who had fallen asleep were raised. ⁵³And coming forth from their tombs after his resurrection,

---

meant to be a deterrent. Matthew focuses on how to make meaning of this horrible death. He uses the Scriptures, primarily the lament psalms, to interpret each action. In verse 35 the division of Jesus' clothing alludes to Psalm 22:18. The wagging heads of the mockers (v. 39) recalls Psalm 22:7.

For the third time (26:67-68; 27:27-31) Jesus endures mockery. First the passers-by (vv. 39-40) resurrect the charge made before the Sanhedrin (26:61) about the destruction of the temple, an event that Matthew connects with the death of Jesus (21:41, 43). Their taunt, "If you are the Son of God," recalls the same tempting words of Satan (4:3, 6), who urges Jesus to throw himself from the pinnacle of the temple and let God's angels rescue him to prove he is truly God's Son. Both scenes reflect the struggle of believers to explain how Jesus can be the beloved Son of God (2:15; 3:17; 17:5) and yet die such a horrendous death. The taunt of the chief priests, scribes, and elders is a variation of the same (vv. 41-42). The paradox of saving life by losing life (16:25) is visibly played out. It is through losing his life that Jesus "saves his people from their sins" (1:21). While the placard over the cross (v. 37) carries the title "King of the Jews" (the charge made by Pilate, 27:11, and his soldiers, 27:29), the religious leaders use the more messianically charged phrase "King of Israel" (v. 42). Verse 43, unique to Matthew, employs Psalm 22:8 and Wisdom 2:18 to align Jesus with the righteous sufferer whom God will vindicate. Finally, even the bandits crucified with Jesus join in the abuse (v. 44; cf. Luke 23:40-43).

27:45-56 Death of Jesus

An apocalyptic tone is set as darkness spreads over the land for three hours (see Amos 8:9). Jesus cries out in a loud voice (v. 46), once again using the words of Psalm 22. He has been deserted and opposed by Judas (26:14-16, 48-49), the disciples (26:56), Peter (26:69-75), the religious lead-

they entered the holy city and appeared to many. [54]The centurion and the men with him who were keeping watch over Jesus feared greatly when they saw the earthquake and all that was happening, and they said, "Truly, this was the Son of God!" [55]There were many women there, looking on from a distance, who had followed Jesus from Galilee, ministering to him. [56]Among them were Mary Magdalene and Mary the mother of James and Joseph, and the mother of the sons of Zebedee.

The Burial of Jesus. [57]When it was evening, there came a rich man from Arimathea named Joseph, who was

---

ers (26:57-68), the crowds (27:21-22), the Roman authorities (27:1-31), and now even God seems to have abandoned him. His anguished prayer is that of a righteous sufferer. While the end of the psalm, which moves to a note of confident hope in God's power to save, is not spoken, the Gospel will indeed end with Jesus' vindication.

The bystanders either misinterpret or deliberately mock Jesus (v. 47) and think he is calling on Elijah. There was an expectation that Elijah would return before the final judgment (Mal 4:5; Sir 48:10). But John the Baptist has already played this role (Matt 11:14; 17:10-13). It is not entirely clear what prompts the offer of *oxos*, a cheap, sour wine used by the lower classes (v. 48), or whether this is a compassionate or mocking gesture. Most likely Matthew includes it as one more way in which Scriptures (Ps 69:21) are fulfilled. As terse as the notice of Jesus' crucifixion (v. 35) is the statement he "gave up his spirit" (v. 50). This is not a reference to the Holy Spirit but to the life-breath (*pneuma* means both "spirit" and "breath") that Jesus hands back to God. Matthew portrays Jesus not as an unwilling victim but as faithful Son of God who consciously returns to God.

Four apocalyptic signs follow immediately, powerful demonstrations that God did not abandon Jesus:

1) The curtain of the temple, probably the inner veil in front of the holy of holies (Exod 26:31-35), is torn (the passive voice designates this as God's doing) from top to bottom. This can be understood as a portent of the destruction of the temple or as opening access to the God of Israel to all the Gentiles.

2) The earth quakes, a portent of the end of the present age and the beginning of the new (4 Ezra 6:13-16; 2 *Apoc. Bar.* 27:7; 70:8; Zech 14:4-5; Matt 24:7). Cosmic signs accompany the momentous events of Jesus' birth (2:2), his death, his resurrection (28:2), and his return in glory (24:27-31).

3) Many of the holy dead emerge from their tombs and appear to people in Jerusalem (vv. 52-53). In verse 52, Matthew, in language akin to

himself a disciple of Jesus. [58]He went to Pilate and asked for the body of Jesus; then Pilate ordered it to be handed over. [59]Taking the body, Joseph wrapped it [in] clean linen [60]and laid it in his new tomb that he had hewn in the rock. Then he rolled a huge stone across the entrance to the tomb and departed. [61]But Mary Magdalene and the other Mary remained sitting there, facing the tomb.

The Guard at the Tomb. [62]The next day, the one following the day of preparation, the chief priests and the Pharisees gathered before Pilate [63]and said, "Sir, we remember that this impostor while still alive said, 'After three days I

---

that of Ezekiel 37, asserts that it is Jesus' death that makes possible the resurrection of the holy ones. The sequence of events becomes confused in verse 53 because Matthew makes a correction: the resurrection of others cannot happen until the resurrection of Jesus, which Matthew has not yet narrated.

4) The centurion and those with him, who had participated in crucifying Jesus, come to believe in Jesus and declare, "Truly this was the Son of God!" (v. 54; cf. vv. 40, 43). This is all the more significant when their employer, the emperor, allocated this title to himself, seeing himself as agent of the gods.

Not only has God not abandoned Jesus but the many Galilean women disciples have also remained faithful to him (vv. 55-56). They are steadfastly keeping watch (as Jesus exhorts disciples to do in chapters 24–25), after having followed Jesus from Galilee and having ministered *(diakonousai)* to him (see 8:15 for various meanings of this verb). Mary Magdalene heads the list (v. 56; as in Matt 27:61; 28:1; Mark 15:40, 47; 16:1, 9; Luke 8:2; 24:10; cf. John 19:25; 20:1-2, 11-18). No information is given about her before this point in the narrative. Only Luke 8:2-3 introduces her before the passion account. The common confusion of her with a prostitute or a sinner has no basis in the Scriptures. The other Mary accompanying her is the mother of James and Joseph (cf. Mark 15:40). At Matthew 13:55 there is the mention of Jesus having siblings named James and Joseph. Possibly Matthew is alluding to the mother of Jesus (cf. John 19:25), but if so, he does not develop the significance. The third figure is the mother of the sons of Zebedee, who at 20:20-21 had wanted places of honor for her sons in Jesus' realm. She drops out of the list in 27:61 and 28:1.

27:57-66 Witnesses at the tomb

Another disciple emerges, a rich man (see 19:16-26, where Jesus elaborates on how difficult it is for a rich person to be a disciple) who offers his tomb for Jesus' burial. There is no mention of Joseph having been part of

will be raised up.' [64]Give orders, then, that the grave be secured until the third day, lest his disciples come and steal him and say to the people, 'He has been raised from the dead.' This last imposture would be worse than the first." [65]Pilate said to them, "The guard is yours; go secure it as best you can." [66]So they went and secured the tomb by fixing a seal to the stone and setting the guard.

28 The Resurrection of Jesus. [1]After the sabbath, as the first day of the week was dawning, Mary Magdalene and the other Mary came to see the tomb. [2]And behold, there was a great earthquake; for an angel of the

---

the Sanhedrin that condemned Jesus (cf. Mark 14:53). There are many limestone quarries in Jerusalem, some of which were used secondarily as cemeteries. A body would be laid in a niche carved in the rock until the flesh decomposed. Then the bones would be gathered into an ossuary ("bone box"), and the niche could be reused for another family member. A tomb complex would have a number of niches. The stone is rolled across the entrance to prevent grave robbers or animals from entering. No anointing of Jesus' body is narrated, since he has already been anointed for burial by an unnamed woman (26:6-13).

Keeping vigil at the tomb (v. 61) are Mary Magdalene and the "other Mary," presumably the mother of James and Joseph named in verse 56. They come again in 28:1 to see the tomb. These witnesses serve to verify that Jesus is truly dead and that there is no mistaking the place of his burial.

Unique to Matthew is the request of the chief priests and the Pharisees (who have been absent since 23:39) to Pilate to set a guard at the tomb (vv. 62-66). Their recollection of Jesus' prediction that after three days he would rise (16:21; 17:23; 20:19) sets the stage for the empty tomb and the resurrection appearances. Their fear of the impact of the disciples' proclamation that Jesus was raised from the dead (v. 64) is ironic, since this is exactly what occurs. The charge that Jesus was an "imposter" (v. 63) and that his disciples stole the body (v. 64) likely reflects the kinds of arguments Matthew's community encountered from their opponents.

28:1-15 The empty tomb

The same two women who witnessed Jesus' crucifixion (27:55-56) and who kept vigil at his burial (27:61) return once again to the tomb. As at the death of Jesus, an earthquake (27:51, 54; see also 24:7), an apocalyptic sign, occurs, accompanied by the descent of an angel from heaven. In the opening chapters an angel conveyed to Joseph the divine interpretation of the puzzling events surrounding Jesus' birth. Similarly, an angel communicates the meaning of the extraordinary aftermath of Jesus' death. In an

Lord descended from heaven, approached, rolled back the stone, and sat upon it. [3]His appearance was like lightning and his clothing was white as snow. [4]The guards were shaken with fear of him and became like dead men. [5]Then the angel said to the women in reply, "Do not be afraid! I know that you are seeking Jesus the crucified. [6]He is not here, for he has been raised just as he said. Come and see the place where he lay. [7]Then go quickly and tell his disciples, 'He has been raised from the dead, and he is going before you to Galilee; there you will see him.' Behold, I have told you." [8]Then they went away quickly from the tomb, fearful yet overjoyed, and ran to announce this to his disciples. [9]And behold, Jesus met them on their way and greeted them. They approached, embraced his feet, and did him homage. [10]Then Jesus said to them, "Do not be afraid. Go tell my brothers to go to Galilee, and there they will see me."

The Report of the Guard. [11]While they were going, some of the guard went into the city and told the chief priests all that had happened. [12]They assembled with the elders and took counsel; then they gave a large sum of money to the soldiers, [13]telling them, "You are to say, 'His disciples came by night and stole him while we were asleep.' [14]And if this gets to the ears of the governor, we will satisfy [him] and keep you out of trouble." [15]The soldiers took the money and did as they were

---

ironic play on words and images, the guards who were supposed to secure the dead body, themselves become like dead men (v. 4).

The angel assures the women not to fear and announces that Jesus has been raised as he said (16:21; 17:22-23; 20:18-19). The passive voice "he has been raised" (v. 6) connotes that God performs the action. The angel then commissions the women to go quickly to give the message to the disciples and to instruct them to go to Galilee, where they will see him (fulfilling Jesus' words in 26:32). Matthew does not explicitly mention Peter (cf. Mark 16:7; Luke 24:12, 34), though he is presumably among the disciples (v. 7) and the Eleven (v. 16). The women do exactly as instructed; with fear and great joy, they run to announce the message to the disciples (v. 8; cf. Mark 16:8, where they say nothing because of their fear).

Unique to Matthew are verses 9-10, where Jesus meets the women on the way. That they seize his feet is a detail that attests to the reality of his person and his tangibility. He is not a ghost or a spirit; nor is it simply the memory of Jesus that lives on with them. The women worship (*proskynein*) Jesus (see also 2:8, 11; 14:33; 15:25; 28:17). Jesus' repetition in verse 10 of the message they have already received from the angel (v. 7) is significant in that the women are commissioned directly by Jesus, giving them credentials as prime witnesses and apostles. Matthew's account represents a

The Church of the Holy Sepulchre in Jerusalem

instructed. And this story has circulated among the Jews to the present [day].

The Commissioning of the Disciples. ◄ ¹⁶The eleven disciples went to Galilee, to the mountain to which Jesus had ordered them. ◄ ¹⁷When they saw him, they worshiped, but they doubted. ¹⁸Then Jesus approached and said to ► them, "All power in heaven and on earth has been given to me. ¹⁹Go, therefore, ► and make disciples of all nations, baptizing them in the name of the Father, and

---

strand of Christian tradition in the same line as that of John 20:1-2, 11-18, where Mary Magdalene goes to the tomb alone and there encounters the risen Christ and is commissioned to announce the good news to the community of brothers and sisters (20:17). By contrast, in Mark 16:1-8 and Luke 24:1-12 the women do not encounter Jesus but only the angel. Peter is given primacy of place by Luke (24:12, 34) and Paul, who does not list the women among those to whom the risen Christ appeared (1 Cor 15:3-8).

Rounding out the story of the guard at the tomb (27:62-66) is their report to the chief priests of all that had happened (28:11-15). Along with the elders, they gather and take counsel (as 27:1). Just as money figured in the plan to hand Jesus over to death (26:14-16; 27:3-10), so did money figure in the false interpretation of his resurrection (v. 12; see 6:19-34; 10:8-9; 13:22; 19:16-30 for warnings about the dangers of money). The ongoing polemics into Matthew's day between followers of Jesus and their opponents are reflected in the remark in verse 15.

FINALE: BACK TO GALILEE; COMMISSION TO THE WHOLE WORLD; JESUS' ABIDING PRESENCE

Matt 28:16-20

28:16-20 The Great Commission

In a scene unique to Matthew, the thread of the story of the women's witness, which left off at verse 10, is resumed. It presumes that they have fulfilled their commission to tell the news of the resurrection to the other disciples and that these have believed them. The juxtaposition of "eleven" with "disciples" creates a tension in the narrative. "Eleven" is a reminder that one of "the Twelve" (see 10:1-4) is no more. Yet "the disciples" (referred to seventy-three times in Matthew) comprised a group larger than the Twelve, among whom were most notably the Galilean women who followed and ministered (27:55). While Matthew has depicted the women as apostles who are commissioned in 28:7-10, he excludes them from the commission to preach to all the nations.

◄ of the Son, and of the holy Spirit, [20]teaching them to observe all that I have commanded you. And behold, I am with you always, until the end of the age."

The mountaintop setting (as at 4:8; 5:1; 15:29; 17:1) evokes the image of Jesus as the new Moses. Like the women (28:9), the Eleven worship Jesus, though unlike them, they (it is not clear in the Greek whether it is all or some of them) doubt or hesitate before the challenge (*distazō*, v. 17; also 14:31). Until this point in the Gospel, Jesus had insisted that the mission was restricted to the "lost sheep of the house of Israel" (10:6; 15:24); now the disciples are to go to "all nations" (*panta ta ethnē*, v. 19; see 25:32). Some understand Matthew to be saying that the mission is to be directed from now on to the Gentiles exclusively (i.e., that the mission to Israel has ended). But more likely Matthew's heavily Jewish Christian community sees that Israel is still included among "all [the] nations" to whom they reach out. The mission is to make disciples, to baptize, and to teach.

A liturgical formula from early Christian tradition has been placed on Jesus' lips (v. 19). As Jesus has been depicted as Teacher par excellence, so are his disciples to follow in his footsteps with his authority (v. 18; see 10:1).

The final verse of the Gospel reiterates the assurance given at 1:23 and 18:20: despite the "little faith" and the failures of his followers, Jesus remains always with the community that gathers and ministers in his name. Not even death can break that bond—ever.

REVIEW AIDS AND DISCUSSION TOPICS

Introduction *(pages 5–10)*

1. Taking into account the likelihood that the author of Matthew was a Jewish Christian writing for a Jewish-Christian community, why does the Gospel contain what appears to be strongly anti-Jewish passages?

2. Since Matthew's Gospel is strongly Jewish in tone and emphasizes the abiding validity of the Law and fulfillment of the Scriptures, what does that say to you about any form of anti-Semitism?

3. Matthew wrote his Gospel at a time when Jewish-Christians had to discern what to keep from their Jewish tradition and what to let go. What cherished traditions have you given up because you saw that changing times demanded this?

1:1–4:11 The Origins of Jesus *(pages 11–29)*

1. What does the presence of the four women in Jesus' genealogy and their unconventional stories say about the role of women in Christianity, in the church?

2. How do Matthew's genealogy and account of Jesus' birth express both continuity and discontinuity with the past?

3. Compare the magi with Herod, the chief priests, and scribes in 2:1-12. Whom do the magi really resemble? In what ways?

4. How does 2:13-23 portray Jesus as a Moses-like figure?

5. Compare John the Baptist and Jesus. How are their messages and missions alike? How do they differ?

6. For Christians of today, what do you think is the most important lesson in Matthew's account of Jesus' baptism?

7. What kind of Son of God is Jesus according to 4:1-11? What types of behavior are rejected as completely objectionable for the Son of God and for Christians?

4:12–10:42 The Beginnings of the Galilean Ministry

4:12-25 Proclamation and Call of the First Disciples *(pages 29–31)*

1. As a Christian, you are a follower of Jesus. What message is there for you in the call of the first disciples?

5:1–7:29 The Sermon on the Mount *(pages 32–49)*

1. What kinds of people are declared "blessed" in 5:3-12? What values in our society do these beatitudes call into question?

2. Do you think Jesus' commands on anger (5:21-26), on nonretaliation (5:38-42), and on love of enemies (5:43-48) are realistic in our world today? Why? As his follower, have you ever acted according to his commands here?

3. What is a common theme in Jesus' commands on almsgiving, prayer, and fasting?

4. What does Jesus' statement "You cannot serve God and mammon" (6:24) say about our accumulating more and more things?

5. In light of the Sermon on the Mount, what kinds of conduct are appropriate for disciples of Jesus? What kinds are inappropriate?

8:1–9:38 Compassionate Healing *(pages 49–59)*

1. What role do faith and prayer play in the miracle stories?

2. What kinds of people are healed by Jesus? What does this say about the scope of his mission? What does it say to you about your mission as a follower of Jesus?

3. What dimensions of Christian discipleship emerge from the three passages (8:18-22; 9:9-17; 9:35-38) that accompany the miracle stories? Have you had to struggle to fulfill some of the demands of such discipleship?

10:1-42 The Mission Discourse *(pages 59–63)*

1. How can genuine disciples of Jesus be distinguished from false disciples? How would you apply this to the different preachers claiming to preach the Good News today?

2. In verses 34-37, Jesus speaks of the strife and division within families that will result from loyalty to him. Have you ever experienced

or known someone who has experienced enmity or ostracism from family members because of faithfulness to Jesus?

3. Today, who are "prophets," "righteous ones," and "little ones"? In what ways can we minister to these disciples?

11:1–16:12 Varying Responses to Jesus

11:1-12:50 Importance and Rejection of Jesus *(pages 65–73)*

1. Why do you think John the Baptist sent his disciples to question Jesus?

2. Why are the Pharisees and scribes so opposed to Jesus in 12:1-14?

3. Why do you think the ordinary people continue to believe in Jesus and follow him while those in authority (Pharisees and scribes) reject and attack him? Can you think of anyone in the church who, like Jesus, was rejected and attacked by church authorities but later shown to be innocent of their charges?

13:1-53 The Parables Discourse *(pages 73–79)*

1. Parables in the Gospels are stories, usually open-ended and puzzling, that allow for a variety of interpretations. Have you found the parables helpful in your life as a follower of Jesus? How?

2. What do you think is the lesson of the wheat and the weeds (vv. 24-30)?

3. What does the parable of the mustard seed say to you about the transformative power of the reign of God? Has such a small "seed" ever revealed God's reign to you? In what way?

4. As a follower of Jesus, have you experienced the joy described in the parables of the buried treasure (v. 44) and the pearl of great price (vv. 45-46)? When?

13:34–16:12 Rejection, Miracles, and Controversy *(pages 79–86)*

1. How do the rejection and execution of John the Baptist (13:54–14:12) point toward the rejection and execution of Jesus?

2. In what ways do the feedings of the five thousand (14:13-21) and the four thousand (15:32-38) point toward the Eucharist and the messianic banquet?

3. Have you ever been asked, like Peter (14:22-36), "to walk on the water"? In what way?

4. Why do you think Jesus ignored and then insulted the Canaanite woman (15:21-28)? Do you think Jesus, as a Jew, might have learned something from this pagan woman of great faith? Have you ever learned from a person who belongs to a group many people look down on?

16:13–20:34 Jesus and His Disciples on the Way to Jerusalem

16:13–17:27 The Way to the Cross *(pages 88–92)*

1. What does the reaction of Peter, as leader of the disciples, to Jesus' prediction of his coming passion and death tell us about Peter's and the other disciples' understanding about the nature of Jesus' messiahship (16:21-23)? Do you think Jesus' rebuke of Peter harsh? Why?

2. How do you think the conditions of discipleship (16:24-28) apply to you?

3. What is the significance of Moses' and Elijah's presence at the Transfiguration (17:1-8)? How does Matthew highlight here that Jesus is the new Moses?

4. In what way does the disciples' reaction to Jesus' second prediction of his passion and death differ from the first? Why do you think it has changed?

18:1-35 Life in Community *(pages 92–96)*

1. Whom is Jesus addressing in the first part (vv. 1-14) of his teaching on community? Do you think his instructions are as applicable now as they were in Matthew's day? Do you think they apply to parents as leaders of the family?

2. Do you think Jesus' teaching regarding reconciliation (vv. 15-20) is a good method for today? Why? Do you think it could work in cases of longstanding grudges?

3. How do you think the parable of the unforgiving servant applies to you as a disciple of Jesus?

19:1–20:34 Ministry in Judea *(pages 96–104)*

1. Jesus' words regarding discipleship and possessions (19:16-30) apply to Christians today. In what way are our status symbols—the

cars we drive, the clothes we wear, the houses we live in—obstacles to our giving to the poor and following Jesus?

2. What is the point of the parable of the owner of the vineyard? Do you sometimes find it hard to accept God's generosity, which is lavished on both the good and the bad? How can resentment and envy divide, even destroy, a community?

3. In 20:20-28, Jesus again teaches his disciples how they are to behave in their positions of authority. Do you know of any instances where someone with authority in the church has "lorded it over" members of the local church?

21:1–28:15 Jerusalem: Jesus' Final Days of Teaching in the Temple

21:1–23:39 Growing Opposition to Jesus (pages 104–119)

1. How does Matthew show that Jesus' arrival and first actions in Jerusalem conform to God's will? Can you think of people today who in some places, including churches, are the equivalent of the lame and blind, who were not welcome in the temple?

2. Jesus addresses the three parables in 21:28–22:14 to the religious leaders. Do you think they have lessons for Christians today? If not, why? If so, what are the lessons?

3. In the five controversies in 21:23-27; 22:15-46, how does Jesus silence his opponents and how does he win honor?

4. Name some modern equivalents to the religious showiness of the scribes and Pharisees? How can followers of Jesus avoid such traps?

5. Give some modern equivalents to the practices Jesus condemns in the seven "woes." How can followers of Jesus avoid such hypocrisy?

24:1–25:46 The Apocalyptic Discourse (pages 119–127)

1. Today we see all the signs of the beginning of the end times that Jesus speaks of. Do you think they necessarily mean that the second coming is near? What does Jesus say about the time and hour of the final judgement?

2. What images are used to express the suddenness of the Human One's coming? What images express his delay?

3. Which of the images or parables in 24:32–25:13 do you think best expresses the importance, the urgency of "staying awake," "being watchful"? How do you "stay awake" and "remain watchful"?

4. What connection is there between the coming of the Human One and the last judgment? What standards will be used in the last judgment? What do those standards say about our lives as followers of Jesus?

5. If "all the nations" are the Gentiles and "the least" are Christians, is the last judgment scene without relevance for Christians today? If no, why? If yes, does it have any relevance regarding our treatment of non-Christians? What about Christians and their actions?

26:1–28:15 The passion and resurrection *(pages 127–146)*

1. How does Matthew show that all the events from the anointing of Jesus at Bethany (26:6-13) to the signs following Jesus death on the cross (27:51-53) were in fulfillment of the Scriptures?

2. What does the disciples' sleeping (26:36-46) after Jesus tells them to "watch and pray" tell you about their understanding of the images and parables in chapters 24–25 and of Jesus' instruction that they pray to be delivered from the test (v. 41; 6:13)? Have you ever found yourself forgetting Jesus' instructions?

3. What are the similarities between Jesus' interrogation before the Sanhedrin (26:57-68) and his trial before Pilate (27:11-31)? Who do you think those who called for Jesus' death were? Why?

4. Do you sympathize with Peter in his denial of Jesus and in his sorrow afterwards? How do you think you would have reacted in his place? How do you think we might deny Jesus today?

5. Why do you think the angel announces Jesus' resurrection to the women and Jesus first appears to them rather than to the male disciples (28:1-10)?

28:16-20 Finale: Back to Galilee; Commission to the Whole World; Jesus' Abiding Presence *(pages 146–147)*

1. Jesus told his disciples to make disciples of all nations (v. 19). As a baptized Christian, do you think this command applies to you? If

so, how do you think you fulfill or can fulfill the command? If not, why?

2. How do you think Jesus remains with the Christian community today?

INDEX OF CITATIONS FROM THE
CATECHISM OF THE CATHOLIC CHURCH

The arabic number(s) following the citation refer to the paragraph number(s) in the *Catechism of the Catholic Church*. The asterisk following a paragraph number indicates that the citation has been paraphrased.

17:23	554*	21:18	544*		679,* 1038
17:24-27	586*	21:22	2610	25:32	1038
18:3-4	526*	21:28-32	546*	25:36	1503
18:3	2785	21:32	535*	25:40	678, 1397,*
18:6	2285	21:33-43 & par.	755*		1825,* 1932, 2449*
18:10	329, 336*	21:34-36	443*	25:41	1034
18:14	605, 2822*	21:37-38	443*	25:45	598,* 1825,*
18:16	2472*	21:42 & par.	756*		2463
18:18	553,* 1444*	21:1-14	546,* 796*	25:46	1038
18:20	1088, 1373	22:21	2242	26:17-29	1339*
18:21-22	982,* 2227,*	22:23-34	575*	26:20	610*
	2845*	22:23-24	581*	26:26	1328, 1329*
18:23-35	2843*	22:34-36	581*	26:28	545, 610, 613,
19:1-12	2364*	22:36	2055		1365, 1846, 2839*
19:3-12	1620*	22:37-40	2055	26:29	1403
19:3-9	2382*	22:37	2083	26:31	764*
19:4	1652	22:40	1824*	26:36-44	2849*
19:6-12	2053*	22:41-46	439,* 447*	26:38	363*
19:6	796, 1605,	23:9	2367*	26:39	536,* 612
	1614, 2336,* 2380*	23:12	526*	26:40	2719*
19:7-9	2382*	23:16-22	2111*	26:41	2733, 2846*
19:8	1610,* 1614*	23:21	586*	26:42	612*
19:10	1615*	23:37a	558*	26:52	2262
19:11	1615*	23:37b	558	26:53	333,* 609*
19:12	922, 1579, 1618	23:39	674	26:54	600*
19:16-19	2052	24:1-2	585*	26:64-66	591*
19:16-17	2075	24:3	585*	26:64	443*
19:18	2400	24:12	675*	26:66	596
19:21	2053*	24:13	161	27:25	597
19:23-29	2053*	24:36	443*	27:39-40	585*
19:23-24	226*	24:44	673*	27:48	515*
19:26	276, 308,* 1058	25:1-13	672,* 796*	27:51	586*
19:28	765*	25:1	672*	27:52-53	633*
20:19	572	25:6	1618*	27:54	441*
20:26	2235	25:13	672*	27:56	500*
20:28	440, 601,* 605,	25:14-30	546,* 1936*	28:1	500, 2174,
	622, 786	25:21	1029,* 1720,*		2174*
20:30	439*		2683*	28:6	652*
21:1-11	559*	25:23	1029,* 1720*	28:9-10	641*
21:9	439*	25:31-46	544,* 1033,*	28:9	645*
21:13	584*		1373, 2447,* 2831*	28:10	654
21:15-16	559*	25:31-36	2443*	28:11-15	640*
21:15	439*	25:31	331, 671,*	28:16-20	857,* 1444*

Index of Citations from the Catechism of the Catholic Church

Palestine in the Time of Jesus

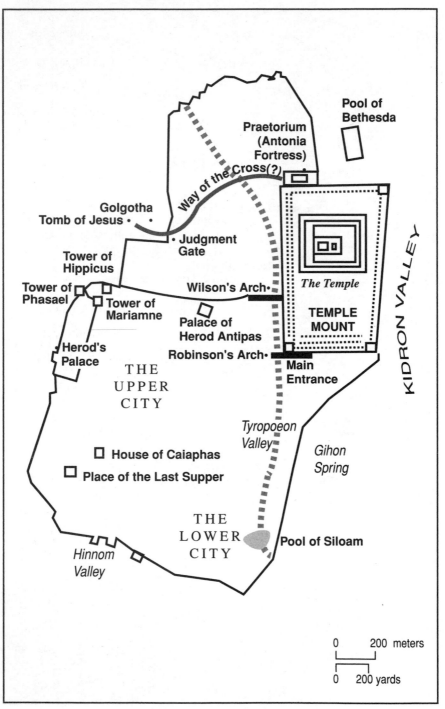

Pool of
Bethesda

Praetorium
(Antonia
Fortress)

Way of the Cross(?)

Golgotha
Tomb of Jesus •   •

• Judgment
Gate

Tower of
Hippicus

The Temple

Tower of
Phasael

Wilson's Arch •

Tower of
Mariamne

TEMPLE
MOUNT

Palace of
Herod Antipas

Robinson's Arch •

Herod's
Palace

Main
Entrance

THE
UPPER
CITY

Tyropoeon
Valley

Gihon
Spring

☐ House of Caiaphas

☐ Place of the Last Supper

THE
LOWER
CITY

Pool of Siloam

Hinnom
Valley

KIDRON VALLEY

0   200 meters

0   200 yards

Jerusalem in the Time of Jesus